BARTLETT'S
BIBLE
QUOTATIONS

BARTLETT'S
BIBLE
QUOTATIONS

John Bartlett

Foreword by Bruce Feiler

Little, Brown and Company

NEW YORK   BOSTON

Little, Brown and Company
Time Warner Book Group
1271 Avenue of the Americas, New York, NY 10020
Visit our Web site at www.twbookmark.com

First Edition: October 2005

The quotations in this book are from *Bartlett's Familiar Quotations*, Seventeenth Edition, Justin Kaplan, General Editor

Library of Congress Cataloging-in-Publication Data

Bible, English. Authorized. Selections. 2005
    Bartlett's Bible quotations / John Bartlett ; Foreword by Bruce Feiler. — 1st ed.
        p. cm.
    "The quotes . . . appeared in Bartlett's familiar quotations, seventeenth edition" — T.p. verso.
        ISBN 0-316-01420-6
        1. Bible — Quotations.   I. Title: Bible quotations.
II. Bartlett, John, 1820–1905.   III. Feiler, Bruce.   IV. Bartlett, John, 1820–1905. Familiar quotations.   V. Title.

BS391.3.B37 2005
220.5'2036 — dc22   2005044340

10   9   8   7   6   5   4   3   2   1

Q-FF

Printed in the United States of America

Contents

The Apocrypha

The New Testament

Foreword

About halfway down the Sinai Peninsula, between Egypt and Israel, lie the ruins of a rock-hewn temple known as Serabit el-Khadim, or "Heights of the Slave." Built on a mountaintop in the early second millennium B.C.E., Serabit el-Khadim represents an attempt by the pharaohs to control workers in nearby turquoise mines. A short walk away is a small cave. To enter, you must lie on your back and slide down a red clay chute into a cavern about the size of the space underneath a pickup truck. On the walls are a handful of inscriptions that are animal-like or anthropoid: snake, ox, fish, house.

Deciphered in 1940 by William Albright, these inscriptions are believed to be the initial forms of a Semitic alphabet, the precursor to our alphabet, and to all alphabets. The snake would become the N, the fish the D, the house the B. These letters, called the protosinaitic inscriptions, are the oldest letters ever found.

Visiting this site a few years ago, I was struck by the fact that the Semitic alphabet was developed in the Ancient Near East in the middle of the second millennium B.C.E., at nearly the exact time that the Israelites would have been traversing this same route during their Exodus from Egypt. Suddenly, the importance of words in the Bible took on new meaning.

Early biblical figures such as Noah, Abraham, and Joseph would have interacted with God, but only orally. By the time of Moses, who would have been born around 1300 B.C.E., this reality would have changed. A great leader would have been able to read. Sure enough, the Ten Commandments, delivered by God on Mount Sinai in a location likely within walking distance of Serabit el-Khadim, are the first words in the Bible that are actually *written down*.

The People of the Book is born.

Written narrative in Israelite religion is one of its chief innovations — and surely one of the principal reasons biblical religion endures to this day. As this collection of biblical quotations makes clear, once stories, prayers, and divine pleas are written down, they can seize the imaginations of nations, transform the world, and even change how people speak.

In 1855, John Bartlett, the owner of the Harvard University bookstore and a well-known trivia buff around Cambridge, Massachusetts, self-published *A Collection of Familiar Quotations*, a book of prose and verse quotes from 169 different authors, which he described as an effort to trace common phrases back to their original sources. The first edition was regularly reprinted and expanded, often imitated, but never equaled, until it became nearly as common in American households as, well, the Bible. I can remember as a self-important teenager poring over *Bartlett's*, looking for quotations to sprinkle into student council speeches and a quote for my high school yearbook.

As they were in John Bartlett's original edition, quotations from the Bible represent the second-largest single block in *Bartlett's* today (the largest is drawn from the works of Shakespeare), and those selections have now been gathered in an edition devoted solely to Scripture. All quotations come from the Authorized Version of the Bible, known as the King James Version, or KJV, published in 1611. The KJV was commissioned by James I of England in 1604 to settle various religious disagreements that had arisen in the century since Martin Luther triggered the Protestant Reformation. The KJV is surely the most influential book ever published in the English language.

Both the weaknesses and strengths of the King James Bible, translated by fifty-four scholars across England, are on display in this volume. The nearly forty books of the Hebrew Bible are here called the Old Testament, a term that has been losing favor in recent years, as it implies that the wisdom of the early books of the Bible was supplanted by the New Testament. Also, the ornate Elizabethan language can sometimes make the Bible seem remote. Genesis 8:11, when the dove Noah sends to survey the flood returns, is rendered here as "And, lo, in her mouth was an olive leaf pluckt off." Exodus 3:5, when Moses encounters God in the burning bush, appears as "Put off thy shoes from off thy feet, for the place whereon thou standest is holy ground." The New Revised Standard Version offers the same line as "Remove the sandals from your feet, for the place on which you are standing is holy ground."

But the towering contributions of the KJV also appear here, and they include some of the most enduring phrases in the English language: "Am I my brother's keeper?"; "pillar of salt"; "coat of many colors"; "Let my people go"; "Man doth not live by bread alone"; "out of the mouth of babes"; "the meek shall inherit the earth"; "They shall beat their swords into plowshares"; "The wolf shall dwell with the lamb"; "Love your enemies"; "Our Father which art in heaven, Hallowed be thy name." Make no mistake: Many of these phrases are translated differently in other editions of the Bible. They were introduced by the King James Bible, picked up in English vernacular, and entered popular imagination. One unexpected gift of *Bartlett's Bible Quotations* is finding these familiar phrases gathered all in one place and seeing them traced, as John Bartlett wished, back to their original source.

Among the quotations assembled here, the book includes what is arguably the most important phrase in Western civilization, a quotation from Genesis 1, "And God said, Let us make man in our image, after our likeness." Early Christians used this line to help weaken the Roman Empire by claiming that society was based not on divine rulers but on the inherent rights of every human being. Centuries later, when the American colonists went looking for a metaphor to express their frustration with British imperial rule, they looked back to this phrase, too. The stirring words of American Creation — "We hold these truths to be self-evident, that all men are created equal, that they are endowed by their Creator with certain unalienable Rights" — are a direct echo of the words of biblical Creation, "Let us make man in our image."

Above all, what the phrases, sentences, psalms, and proverbs gathered in *Bartlett's Bible Quotations* demonstrate is an idea as old as the first few lines of Genesis.

> In the beginning God created the heaven
> and the earth.
> And the earth was without form, and void; and
> darkness was upon the face of the deep. And the Spirit
> of God moved upon the face of the waters.
> And God said, Let there be light: and there was light.

"And God said." The Bible introduced the notion that millennia later countless sermons, study groups, private reading sessions, scholarly interpretations, and books like this reinforce. The most powerful force in the world — the one God himself employs to create the world — is not earth, water, fire, or light.

It is words.

Bruce Feiler

BARTLETT'S
BIBLE
QUOTATIONS

The Old Testament

THE FIRST BOOK OF MOSES, CALLED GENESIS

In the beginning God created the heaven
and the earth.
And the earth was without form, and void; and
darkness was upon the face of the deep. And the Spirit
of God moved upon the face of the waters.
And God said, Let there be light: and there was light.

Chapter 1, verses 1–3

And the evening and the morning were the
first day. *1:5*

And God saw that it was good. *1:10*

And God said, Let us make man in our image, after
our likeness. *1:26*

Male and female created he them. *1:27*

Be fruitful, and multiply, and replenish the earth, and
subdue it: and have dominion over the fish of the sea,
and over the fowl of the air, and over every living
thing that moveth upon the earth. *1:28*

And on the seventh day God ended his work which
he had made. 2:2

And the Lord God formed man of the dust of the
ground, and breathed into his nostrils the breath of
life; and man became a living soul. 2:7

And the Lord God planted a garden eastward
in Eden. 2:8

The tree of life also in the midst of the garden. 2:9

But of the tree of the knowledge of good and evil,
thou shalt not eat of it: for in the day that thou eatest
thereof thou shalt surely die. 2:17

It is not good that the man should be alone; I will
make him an help meet for him. 2:18

And the Lord God caused a deep sleep to fall upon
Adam, and he slept: and he took one of his ribs, and
closed up the flesh instead thereof.
And the rib, which the Lord God had taken from
man, made he a woman. 2:21–22

Bone of my bones, and flesh of my flesh. 2:23

Therefore shall a man leave his father and his
mother, and shall cleave unto his wife: and they
shall be one flesh.
And they were both naked, the man and his wife, and
were not ashamed. 2:24–25

Now the serpent was more subtile than any beast of
the field. 3:1

Your eyes shall be opened, and ye shall be as gods,
knowing good and evil. 3:5

And they sewed fig leaves together, and made
themselves aprons.
And they heard the voice of the Lord God walking in
the garden in the cool of the day. 3:7–8

The woman whom thou gavest to be with me, she
gave me of the tree, and I did eat. 3:12

What is this that thou hast done? And the woman
said, The serpent beguiled me, and I did eat.
And the Lord God said unto the serpent, Because thou
hast done this, thou art cursed above all cattle, and
above every beast of the field; upon thy belly shalt
thou go, and dust shalt thou eat all the days of thy
life. 3:13–14

And I will put enmity between thee and the woman,
and between thy seed and her seed; it shall bruise thy
head, and thou shalt bruise his heel.   3:15

In sorrow thou shalt bring forth children.   3:16

In the sweat of thy face shalt thou eat bread, till thou
return unto the ground; for out of it wast thou taken:
for dust thou art, and unto dust shalt thou return.
And Adam called his wife's name Eve; because she was
the mother of all living.   3:19–20

So he drove out the man: and he placed at the east of
the garden of Eden cherubims, and a flaming sword
which turned every way, to keep the way of the tree
of life.   3:24

And Abel was a keeper of sheep, but Cain was a tiller
of the ground.   4:2

Am I my brother's keeper?   4:9

The voice of thy brother's blood crieth unto me from
the ground.   4:10

A fugitive and a vagabond shalt thou be in the earth.

4:12

My punishment is greater than I can bear. 4:13

And the Lord set a mark upon Cain. 4:15

And Cain went out from the presence of the Lord,
and dwelt in the land of Nod. 4:16

Jabal: he was the father of such as dwell in tents. 4:20

Jubal: he was the father of all such as handle the harp
and organ. 4:21

Tubal-cain, an instructor of every artificer in brass and
iron. 4:22

And Enoch walked with God. 5:24

And all the days of Methuselah were nine hundred
sixty and nine years. 5:27

And Noah begat Shem, Ham, and Japheth. 5:32

There were giants in the earth in those days . . . mighty
men which were of old, men of renown. 6:4

Make thee an ark of gopher wood. 6:14

And of every living thing of all flesh, two of every sort
shalt thou bring into the ark. 6:19

And the rain was upon the earth forty days and forty
nights. 7:12

But the dove found no rest for the sole of her foot. 8:9

And, lo, in her mouth was an olive leaf pluckt off. 8:11

For the imagination of man's heart is evil from his
youth. 8:21

While the earth remaineth, seedtime and harvest, and
cold and heat, and summer and winter, and day and
night shall not cease. 8:22

Whoso sheddeth man's blood, by man shall his blood
be shed: for in the image of God made he man. 9:6

I do set my bow in the cloud, and it shall be for a
token of a covenant between me and the earth. *9:13*

Even as Nimrod the mighty hunter before
the Lord. *10:9*

Therefore is the name of it called Babel; because the
Lord did there confound the language of all the earth.
11:9

Let there be no strife, I pray thee, between me and
thee . . . for we be brethren. *13:8*

Abram dwelled in the land of Canaan, and Lot
dwelled in the cities of the plain, and pitched his tent
toward Sodom. *13:12*

In a good old age. *15:15*

His [Ishmael's] hand will be against every man, and
every man's hand against him. *16:12*

Thy name shall be Abraham; for a father of many
nations have I made thee. *17:5*

My Lord, if now I have found favor in thy sight, pass
not away, I pray thee, from thy servant. 18:3

But his [Lot's] wife looked back from behind him, and
she became a pillar of salt. 19:26

My son, God will provide himself a lamb for a burnt
offering. 22:8

Behold behind him a ram caught in a thicket by his
horns. 22:13

Esau was a cunning hunter, a man of the field; and
Jacob was a plain man, dwelling in tents. 25:27

And he [Esau] sold his birthright unto Jacob.
Then Jacob gave Esau bread and pottage of lentils.
25:33–34

The voice is Jacob's voice, but the hands are the hands
of Esau. 27:22

Thy brother came with subtilty, and hath taken away
thy blessing. 27:35

He [Jacob] dreamed, and behold a ladder set up on the earth, and the top of it reached to heaven: and behold the angels of God ascending and descending on it. 28:12

Surely the Lord is in this place; and I knew it not. 28:16

This is none other but the house of God, and this is the gate of heaven. 28:17

Jacob served seven years for Rachel; and they seemed unto him but a few days, for the love he had to her. 29:20

And Laban said, This heap [of stones] is a witness between me and thee this day. Therefore was the name of it called Galeed; And Mizpah; for he said, The Lord watch between me and thee, when we are absent one from another. 31:48–49

And Jacob was left alone; and there wrestled a man with him until the breaking of the day. 32:24

I will not let thee go, except thou bless me. 32:26

And Jacob called the name of the place Peniel:
for I have seen God face to face, and my life
is preserved. 32:30

Behold, this dreamer cometh. 37:19

They stript Joseph out of his coat, his coat of
many colors. 37:23

The Lord made all that he did to prosper in
his hand. 39:3

And she [Potiphar's wife] caught him by his garment,
saying, Lie with me: and he left his garment in her
hand, and fled, and got him out. 39:12

The seven good kine are seven years; and the seven
good ears are seven years: the dream is one.
And the seven thin and ill-favored kine that came up
after them are seven years; and the seven empty ears
blasted with the east wind shall be seven years of
famine. 41:26–27

Then shall ye bring down my gray hairs with sorrow
to the grave. 42:38

But Benjamin's mess was five times so much as any
of theirs. 43:34

Wherefore have ye rewarded evil for good? 44:4

God forbid. 44:7

The man in whose hand the cup is found, he shall be
my servant. 44:17

And he fell upon his brother Benjamin's neck, and
wept; and Benjamin wept upon his neck. 45:14

And ye shall eat the fat of the land. 45:18

And they came into the land of Goshen. 46:28

But I will lie with my fathers, and thou shalt carry me
out of Egypt, and bury me in their buryingplace. And
he said, I will do as thou hast said. 47:30

Unstable as water, thou shalt not excel. 49:4

I have waited for thy salvation, O Lord. 49:18

Unto the utmost bound of the everlasting hills. 49:26

THE SECOND BOOK OF MOSES, CALLED EXODUS

Now there arose up a new king over Egypt, which knew not Joseph. 1:8

She took for him an ark of bulrushes, and daubed it with slime and with pitch. 2:3

I have been a stranger in a strange land. 2:22

Behold, the bush burned with fire, and the bush was not consumed. 3:2

Put off thy shoes from off thy feet, for the place whereon thou standest is holy ground. 3:5

And Moses hid his face; for he was afraid to look upon God. 3:6

A land flowing with milk and honey. 3:8

And God said unto Moses, I AM THAT I AM. 3:14

I am slow of speech, and of a slow tongue. 4:10

Let my people go. 5:1

Ye shall no more give the people straw to
make brick. 5:7

Thou shalt say unto Aaron, Take thy rod, and cast it
before Pharaoh, and it shall become a serpent. 7:9

They [Pharaoh's wise men] cast down every man his
rod, and they became serpents: but Aaron's rod
swallowed up their rods.
And he hardened Pharaoh's heart. 7:12–13

This is the finger of God. 8:19

Darkness which may be felt. 10:21

Yet will I bring one plague more upon Pharaoh, and
upon Egypt. 11:1

Your lamb shall be without blemish. 12:5

And they shall eat the flesh in that night, roast with fire, and unleavened bread; and with bitter herbs they shall eat it. *12:8*

And thus shall ye eat it; with your loins girded, your shoes on your feet, and your staff in your hand; and ye shall eat it in haste: it is the Lord's passover. For I will pass through the land of Egypt this night, and will smite all the firstborn in the land of Egypt, both man and beast; and against all the gods of Egypt I will execute judgment: I am the Lord. *12:11–12*

This day [Passover] shall be unto you for a memorial; and ye shall keep it a feast to the Lord throughout your generations. *12:14*

Seven days shall ye eat unleavened bread. *12:15*

There was a great cry in Egypt; for there was not a house where there was not one dead. *12:30*

Remember this day, in which ye came out from Egypt, out of the house of bondage. *13:3*

And the Lord went before them by day in a pillar of a
cloud, to lead them the way; and by night in a pillar
of fire, to give them light. *13:21*

And the children of Israel went into the midst of the
sea upon the dry ground: and the waters were a wall
unto them on their right hand, and on their left. *14:22*

I will sing unto the Lord, for he hath triumphed
gloriously: the horse and his rider hath he thrown
into the sea.
The Lord is my strength and song, and he is become
my salvation. *15:1-2*

The Lord is a man of war. *15:3*

Thy right hand, O Lord, is become glorious in power:
thy right hand, O Lord, hath dashed in pieces the
enemy. *15:6*

Thou sentest forth thy wrath, which consumed them
as stubble.
And with the blast of thy nostrils the waters were
gathered together, the floods stood upright as an
heap, and the depths were congealed in the heart of
the sea. *15:7-8*

Would to God we had died by the hand of the Lord in
the land of Egypt, when we sat by the fleshpots, and
when we did eat bread to the full. 16:3

It is manna. 16:15

I am the Lord thy God. 20:2

Thou shalt have no other gods before me.
Thou shalt not make unto thee any graven
image. 20:3–4

For I the Lord thy God am a jealous God, visiting the
iniquity of the fathers upon the children unto the
third and fourth generation of them that hate me;
And showing mercy unto thousands of them that love
me, and keep my commandments.
Thou shalt not take the name of the Lord thy God
in vain. 20:5–7

Remember the sabbath day, to keep it holy.
Six days shalt thou labor, and do all thy work:
But the seventh day . . . thou shalt not do any
work. 20:8–10

Honor thy father and thy mother: that thy days may
be long upon the land which the Lord thy God
giveth thee.
Thou shalt not kill.
Thou shalt not commit adultery.
Thou shalt not steal.
Thou shalt not bear false witness against thy
neighbor.
Thou shalt not covet thy neighbor's house, thou shalt
not covet thy neighbor's wife, nor his manservant, nor
his maidservant, nor his ox, nor his ass, nor any thing
that is thy neighbor's. 20:12–17

But let not God speak with us, lest we die. 20:19

He that smiteth a man, so that he die, shall be surely
put to death. 21:12

Eye for eye, tooth for tooth, hand for hand, foot for
foot. 21:24

Behold, I send an Angel before thee, to keep thee in
the way. 23:20

A stiffnecked people. 32:9

Who is on the Lord's side? let him come unto me. 32:26

Thou canst not see my face: for there shall no man see
me, and live. 33:20

And he [Moses] was there with the Lord forty days
and forty nights; he did neither eat bread, nor drink
water. And he wrote upon the tables the words of the
covenant, the ten commandments. 34:28

THE THIRD BOOK OF MOSES, CALLED LEVITICUS

Whatsoever parteth the hoof, and is cloven-footed,
and cheweth the cud, among the beasts, that
shall ye eat. 11:3

And the swine   , is unclean to you.
Of their flesh shall ye not cut 11:7-8

Let him go for a scapegoat into the wilderness. 16:10

And when ye reap the harvest of your land, thou shalt
not wholly reap the corners of thy field, neither shalt
thou gather the gleanings of thy harvest.
And thou shalt not glean thy vineyard, neither shalt
thou gather every grape of thy vineyard; thou shalt
leave them for the poor and stranger. 19:9–10

u shalt not go up and down as a talebearer among
thy people. *19:16*

Thou shalt love thy neighbor as thyself. *19:18*

Ye shall hallow the fiftieth year, and proclaim liberty
throughout all the land unto all the inhabitants
thereof: it shall be a jubilee unto you. *25:10*

THE FOURTH BOOK OF MOSES, CALLED NUMBERS

The Lord bless thee, and keep thee:
The Lord make his face shine upon thee, and be
gracious unto thee:
The Lord lift up his countenance upon thee, and give
thee peace. *6:24–26*

Sent to spy out the land. *13:16*

And your children shall wander in the wilderness forty
years. *14:33*

ed up his hand, and with his rod he smote
and the water came
tly. *20:11*

He whom thou blessest is blessed. 22:6

The Lord opened the mouth of the ass, and she said unto Balaam, What have I done unto thee? 22:28

Let me die the death of the righteous, and let my last end be like his! 23:10

God is not a man, that he should lie. 23:19

What hath God wrought! 23:23

How goodly are thy tents, O Jacob, and thy tabernacles, O Israel! 24:5

Be sure your sin will find you out. 32:23

THE FIFTH BOOK OF MOSES, CALLED DEUTERONOMY

I call heaven and earth to witness. 4:26

Hear, O Israel: The Lord our God is one Lord.

Thou shalt love the Lord thy God with all thine heart,
and with all thy soul, and with all thy might.
And these words, which I command thee this day,
shall be in thine heart:
And thou shalt teach them diligently unto thy
children. 6:5–7

Ye shall not tempt the Lord your God. 6:16

The Lord thy God hath chosen thee to be a special
people unto himself. 7:6

Man doth not live by bread only, but by every word
that proceedeth out of the mouth of the Lord doth
man live. 8:3

For the Lord thy God bringeth thee into a
good land. 8:7

A land of wheat, and barley, and vines, and fig trees,
and pomegranates; a land of oil olive, and honey;
A land wherein thou shalt eat bread without
scarceness, thou shalt not lack any thing in it; a land
whose stones are iron, and out of whose hills thou
mayest dig brass. 8:8–9

A dreamer of dreams. 13:1

The wife of thy bosom. 13:6

The poor shall never cease out of the land. 15:11

Thou shalt not move a sickle unto thy neighbor's
standing corn. 23:25

Thou shalt not muzzle the ox when he treadeth out
the corn. 25:4

And thou shalt become an astonishment, a proverb,
and a byword, among all nations. 28:37

In the morning thou shalt say, Would God it were
even! and at even thou shalt say, Would God it were
morning! 28:67

The secret things belong unto the Lord our God. 29:29

I have set before you life and death, blessing and
cursing: therefore choose life, that both thou and thy
seed may live. 30:19

He is the Rock, his work is perfect: for all his ways are
judgment: a God of truth. 32:4

Jeshurun waxed fat, and kicked. 32:15

As thy days, so shall thy strength be. 33:25

The eternal God is thy refuge, and underneath are the
everlasting arms. 33:27

No man knoweth of his [Moses'] sepulcher unto
this day. 34:6

THE BOOK OF JOSHUA

Be strong and of a good courage; be not afraid,
neither be thou dismayed: for the Lord thy God is
with thee whithersoever thou goest. 1:9

And the priests that bare the ark of the covenant of
the Lord stood firm on dry ground in the midst of
Jordan, and all the Israelites passed over on dry
ground, until all the people were passed clean over
Jordan. 3:17

Mighty men of valor. 6:2

And it came to pass, when the people heard the sound
of the trumpet, and the people shouted with a great
shout, that the wall fell down flat, so that the people
went up into the city [Jericho]. 6:20

His fame was noised throughout all the country. 6:27

Hewers of wood and drawers of water. 9:21

Sun, stand thou still upon Gibeon; and thou, Moon, in
the valley of Ajalon. 10:12

Old and stricken in years. 13:1

I am going the way of all the earth. 23:14

THE BOOK OF JUDGES

They shall be as thorns in your sides. 2:3

Then Jael, Heber's wife, took a nail of the tent, and
took an hammer in her hand, and went softly unto
him [Sisera], and smote the nail into his temples, and
fastened it into the ground; for he was fast asleep, and
weary: so he died. 4:21

I Deborah arose . . . I arose a mother in Israel. 5:7

Awake, awake, Deborah: awake, awake, utter a song:
arise, Barak, and lead thy captivity captive. 5:12

The stars in their courses fought against Sisera. 5:20

She [Jael] brought forth butter in a lordly dish. 5:25

At her feet he bowed, he fell, he lay down: at her feet
he bowed, he fell: where he bowed, there he fell
down dead. 5:27

The mother of Sisera looked out at a window, and
cried through the lattice, Why is his chariot so long in
coming? why tarry the wheels of his chariots? 5:28

Have they not divided the prey; to every man a
damsel or two? 5:30

The sword of the Lord, and of Gideon. 7:18

Is not the gleaning of the grapes of Ephraim better
than the vintage of Abiezer? 8:2

Say now Shibboleth: and he said Sibboleth: for he
could not frame to pronounce it right. *12:6*

There was a swarm of bees and honey in the carcass of
the lion. *14:8*

Out of the eater came forth meat, and out of the
strong came forth sweetness. *14:14*

If ye had not plowed with my heifer, ye had not found
out my riddle. *14:18*

He smote them hip and thigh. *15:8*

With the jawbone of an ass . . . have I slain a thousand
men. *15:16*

The Philistines be upon thee, Samson. *16:9*

The Philistines took him [Samson], and put out his
eyes, and brought him down to Gaza, and bound him
with fetters of brass; and he did grind in the
prison house. *16:21*

Strengthen me, I pray thee, only this once, O God,
that I may be . . . avenged of the Philistines for my
two eyes. *16:28*

So the dead which he slew at his death were more
than they which he slew in his life. *16:30*

From Dan even to Beersheba. *20:1*

All the people arose as one man. *20:8*

In those days there was no king in Israel: every man
did that which was right in his own eyes *21:25*

THE BOOK OF RUTH

Whither thou goest, I will go; and where thou
lodgest, I will lodge. thy people shall be my people,
and thy God my God. *1:16*

Let me glean and gather after the reapers among the
sheaves. *2:7*

Go not empty unto thy mother in law. *3:17*

THE FIRST BOOK OF SAMUEL

In the flower of their age. 2:33

The Lord called Samuel: and he answered, Here am I.
3:4

Speak, Lord; for thy servant heareth. 3:9

Be strong, and quit yourselves like men. 4:9

And she named the child Ichabod, saying, The glory
is departed from Israel: because the ark of God was
taken. 4:21

Is Saul also among the prophets? 10:11

God save the king. 10:24

A man after his own heart. 13:14

Every man's sword was against his fellow. 14:20

, wherefore should I fast? Can I bring
in? I shall go to him, but he shall not
return to me. 12:23

ls die, and are as water spilt on the
nnot be gathered up again. 14:14

d for thee, O Absalom, my son,
y son! 18:33

, and my fortress, and my
erer. 22:2

he sweet psalmist of Israel.

heir lives. 23:17

HE KINGS

heart. 3:12

a in multitude.

But Jonathan heard not when his father charged the
people with the oath: wherefore he put forth the end
of the rod that was in his hand, and dipped it in an
honeycomb, and put his hand to his mouth; and his
eyes were enlightened. 14:27

For the Lord seeth not as man seeth; for man looketh
on the outward appearance, but the Lord looketh on
the heart. 16:7

I know thy pride, and the naughtiness of
thine heart. 17:20

Let no man's heart fail because of him [Goliath]. 17:32

Go, and the Lord be with thee. 17:37

And he [David] . . . chose him five smooth stones out
of the brook. 17:40

So David prevailed over the Philistine with a sling and
with a stone. 17:50

Saul hath slain his thousands, and David his ten
thousands. 18:7

And Jonathan . . . loved him [David] as he loved his
own soul.   20:17

Wickedness proceedeth from the wicked.   24:13

I have played the fool.   26:21

THE SECOND BOOK OF SAMUEL

Tell it not in Gath, publish it not in the streets
of Askelon.   1:20

Saul and Jonathan were lovely and pleasant in their
lives, and in their death they were not divided: they
were swifter than eagles, they were stronger
than lions.   1:23

How are the mighty fallen in the midst of the battle!
1:25

Thy love to me was wonderful, passing the
love of women.
How are the mighty fallen, and the weapons of war
perished!   1:26–27

Abne·

Knc

Now he is
him back aga

For we must nee
ground, which ca

Would God I had di
m

The Lord is my rock
deliv

David the son of Jesse . . . t

Went in jeopardy of
23:

THE FIRST BOOK OF

A wise and an understandin

Many, as the sand which is by the s
4:20

Judah and Israel dwelt safely, every man under his vine and under his fig tree. 4:25

He [Solomon] spake three thousand proverbs: and his songs were a thousand and five. 4:32

The wisdom of Solomon. 4:34

So that there was neither hammer nor axe nor any tool of iron heard in the house, while it was in building. 6:7

A proverb and a byword among all people. 9:7

When the queen of Sheba heard of the fame of Solomon . . . she came to prove him with hard questions. 10:1

The half was not told me: thy wisdom and prosperity exceedeth the fame which I heard. 10:7

Once in three years came the navy of Tharshish, bringing gold, and silver, ivory, and apes, and peacocks. 10:22

King Solomon loved many strange women. *11:1*

My father hath chastised you with whips, but I will chastise you with scorpions. *12:11*

To your tents, O Israel. *12:16*

He [Elijah] went and dwelt by the brook Cherith, that is before Jordan. *17:5*

And the ravens brought him bread and flesh in the morning, and bread and flesh in the evening; and he drank of the brook. *17:6*

An handful of meal in a barrel, and a little oil in a cruse. *17:12*

And the barrel of meal wasted not, neither did the cruse of oil fail. *17:16*

How long halt ye between two opinions? *18:21*

Either he [Baal] is talking, or he is pursuing, or he is in a journey, or peradventure he sleepeth, and must be awaked. *18:27*

There ariseth a little cloud out of the sea, like a man's
hand. 18:44

And he girded up his loins, and ran before Ahab. 18:46

But the Lord was not in the wind: and after the wind
an earthquake; but the Lord was not in the
earthquake:
And after the earthquake a fire; but the Lord was not
in the fire: and after the fire a still small voice. 19:11–12

Let not him that girdeth on his harness boast himself
as he that putteth it off. 20:11

Hast thou found me, O mine enemy? 21:20

The dogs shall eat Jezebel by the wall of Jezreel. 21:23

But there was none like unto Ahab, which did sell
himself to work wickedness in the sight of the Lord,
whom Jezebel his wife stirred up. 21:25

I saw all Israel scattered upon the hills, as sheep that
have not a shepherd. 22:17

Feed him [Micajah] with bread of affliction, and with
water of affliction, until I come in peace. 22:27

THE SECOND BOOK OF THE KINGS

There appeared a chariot of fire, and horses of fire,
and parted them both asunder; and Elijah went up by
a whirlwind into heaven. 2:11

The chariot of Israel, and the horsemen thereof. And
he saw him no more. 2:12

He [Elisha] took up also the mantle of Elijah. 2:13

There is death in the pot. 4:40

Is thy servant a dog, that he should do this great
thing? 8:13

What hast thou to do with peace? turn thee
behind me. 9:18

The driving is like the driving of Jehu the son of
Nimshi; for he driveth furiously. 9:20

Jezebel heard of it; and she painted her face, and tired
her head, and looked out at a window. 9:30

The angel of the Lord went out, and smote in the
camp of the Assyrians an hundred fourscore and five
thousand: and when they arose early in the morning,
behold, they were all dead corpses.
So Sennacherib king of Assyria departed. 19:35–36

Set thine house in order. 20:1

I will wipe Jerusalem as a man wipeth a dish, wiping it,
and turning it upside down. 21:13

THE FIRST BOOK OF THE CHRONICLES

His mercy endureth for ever. 16:41

The Lord searcheth all hearts, and understandeth all
the imaginations of the thoughts. 28:9

Thine, O Lord, is the greatness, and the power, and
the glory, and the victory, and the majesty: for all that
is in the heaven and in the earth is thine; thine is the
kingdom, O Lord, and thou art exalted as head above
all. 29:11

For all things come of thee, and of thine own have we given thee. 29:14

Our days on the earth are as a shadow. 29:15

He [David] died in a good old age, full of days, riches, and honor. 29:28

THE BOOK OF NEHEMIAH

They which builded on the wall, and they that bare burdens, with those that laded, every one with one of his hands wrought in the work, and with the other hand held a weapon. 4:17

And he [Ezra] read therein before the street that was before the water gate from the morning until midday, before the men and the women, and those that could understand; and the ears of all the people were attentive unto the book of the law. 8:3

Thou art a God ready to pardon, gracious and merciful, slow to anger, and of great kindness. 9:17

THE BOOK OF ESTHER

Mordecai rent his clothes, and put on sackcloth with ashes. 4:1

The man whom the king delighteth to honor. 6:6

They hanged Haman on the gallows. 7:10

THE BOOK OF JOB

One that feared God, and eschewed evil. 1:1

Satan came also. 1:6

And the Lord said unto Satan, Whence comest thou? Then Satan answered the Lord, and said, From going to and fro in the earth, and from walking up and down in it. 1:7

Doth Job fear God for nought? 1:9

And I only am escaped alone to tell thee. 1:15

Naked came I out of my mother's womb, and naked
shall I return thither: the Lord gave, and the Lord hath
taken away; blessed be the name of the Lord. *1:21*

Skin for skin, yea, all that a man hath will he give for
his life. *2:4*

Curse God, and die. *2:9*

Let the day perish wherein I was born, and the
night in which it was said, There is a man
child conceived. *3:3*

For now should I have lain still and been quiet, I
should have slept: then had I been at rest,
With kings and counsellors of the earth, which built
desolate places for themselves. *3:13–14*

There the wicked cease from troubling; and there the
weary be at rest. *3:17*

Who ever perished, being innocent? or where were
the righteous cut off? *4:7*

Fear came upon me, and trembling. *4:14*

Then a spirit passed before my face; the hair of my
flesh stood up. 4:15

Shall mortal man be more just than God? shall a man
be more pure than his maker? 4:17

Wrath killeth the foolish man, and envy slayeth the
silly one. 5:2

Man is born unto trouble, as the sparks fly upward. 5:7

He taketh the wise in their own craftiness. 5:13

For thou shalt be in league with the stones of the
field: and the beasts of the field shall be at peace
with thee. 5:23

Thou shalt come to thy grave in a full age, like as a
shock of corn cometh in in his season. 5:26

How forcible are right words! 6.25

My days are swifter than a weaver's shuttle, and are
spent without hope. 7:6

He shall return no more to his house, neither shall his
place know him any more. 7:10

I would not live alway: let me alone: for my days are
vanity. 7:16

But how should man be just with God? 9:2

The land of darkness and the shadow of death. 10:21

Canst thou by searching find out God? 11:7

And thine age shall be clearer than the noonday. 11:17

No doubt but ye are the people, and wisdom shall die
with you. 12:2

The just upright man is laughed to scorn. 12:4

But ask now the beasts, and they shall teach thee; and
the fowls of the air, and they shall tell thee:
Or speak to the earth, and it shall teach thee; and the
fishes of the sea shall declare unto thee. 12:7–8

With the ancient is wisdom; and in length of days
understanding. *12:12*

He discovereth deep things out of darkness, and
bringeth out to light the shadow of death. *12:22*

Though he slay me, yet will I trust in him. *13:15*

Man that is born of a woman is of few days, and full of
trouble.
He cometh forth like a flower, and is cut down: he
fleeth also as a shadow, and continueth not. *14:1–2*

But man dieth, and wasteth away: yea, man giveth up
the ghost, and where is he? *14.10*

If a man die, shall he live again? *14:14*

Should a wise man utter vain knowledge, and fill his
belly with the east wind? *15:2*

Miserable comforters are ye all. *16:2*

My days are past. *17:11*

I have said to corruption, Thou art my father: to the
worm, Thou art my mother, and my sister. *17:14*

The king of terrors. *18:14*

I am escaped with the skin of my teeth. *19:20*

Oh that my words were now written! oh that they
were printed in a book! *19:23*

I know that my redeemer liveth, and that he shall
stand at the latter day upon the earth:
And though, after my skin, worms destroy this body,
yet in my flesh shall I see God. *19:25–26*

Seeing the root of the matter is found in me. *19:28*

Though wickedness be sweet in his mouth, though he
hide it under his tongue. *20:12*

Suffer me that I may speak; and after that I have
spoken, mock on. *21:3*

Shall any teach God knowledge? *21:22*

They are of those that rebel against the light. 24:13

The womb shall forget him; the worm shall
feed sweetly on him; he shall be no
more remembered. 24:20

Yea, the stars are not pure in his sight.
How much less man, that is a worm? and the son of
man, which is a worm? 25:5–6

But where shall wisdom be found? and where is the
place of understanding? 28:12

The land of the living. 28:13

The price of wisdom is above rubies. 28:18

Behold, the fear of the Lord, that is wisdom; and to
depart from evil is understanding. 28:28

I caused the widow's heart to sing for joy. 29:13

I was eyes to the blind, and feet was I to
the lame. 29:15

I know that thou wilt bring me to death, and to the house appointed for all living. 30:23

I am a brother to dragons, and a companion to owls.
30:29

My desire is, that the Almighty would answer me, and that mine adversary had written a book. 31:35

Great men are not always wise. 32:9

For I am full of matter, the spirit within me constraineth me. 32:18

One among a thousand. 33:23

Far be it from God, that he should do wickedness.
34:10

He multiplieth words without knowledge. 35:16

Fair weather cometh out of the north. 37:22

Then the Lord answered Job out of the whirlwind,
and said,
Who is this that darkeneth counsel by words without
knowledge?
Gird up now thy loins like a man. 38:1–3

Where wast thou when I laid the foundations of the
earth? declare, if thou hast understanding. 38:4

The morning stars sang together, and all the sons of
God shouted for joy. 38:7

Hitherto shalt thou come, but no further: and here
shall thy proud waves be stayed. 38:11

Hast thou entered into the springs of the sea? or hast
thou walked in the search of the depth? 38:16

Hath the rain a father? or who hath begotten the
drops of dew? 38:28

Canst thou bind the sweet influences of Pleiades, or
loose the bands of Orion? 38:31

Canst thou guide Arcturus with his sons? 38:32

Who can number the clouds in wisdom? or who can
stay the bottles of heaven. 38:37

Hast thou given the horse strength? hast thou clothed
his neck with thunder? 39:19

He paweth in the valley, and rejoiceth in his strength:
he goeth on to meet the armed men. 39:21

He swalloweth the ground with fierceness and rage;
neither believeth he that it is the sound of the
trumpet.
He saith among the trumpets, Ha, ha; and he smelleth
the battle afar off, the thunder of the captains, and the
shouting. 39:24–25

Doth the eagle mount up at thy command, and make
her nest on high?
She dwelleth and abideth on the rock, upon the crag
of the rock, and the strong place.
From thence she seeketh the prey, and her eyes
behold afar off.
Her young ones also suck up blood: and where the
slain are, there is she. 39:27–30

Behold, I am vile; what shall I answer thee? 40:4

Behold now behemoth, which I made with thee; he
eateth grass as an ox. 40:15

Canst thou draw out leviathan with a hook? 41:1

Who can open the doors of his face? his teeth are
terrible round about.
His scales are his pride, shut up together as with a
close seal. 41:14–15

His heart is as firm as a stone; yea as hard as a piece of
the nether millstone. 41:24

He maketh the deep to boil like a pot. 41:31

Upon earth there is not his like, who is made without
fear. 41:33

He is a king over all the children of pride 41:34

I have heard of thee by the hearing of the ear: but
now mine eye seeth thee. 42:5

So the Lord blessed the latter end of Job more than
his beginning. 42:12

THE BOOK OF PSALMS

Blessed is the man that walketh not in the counsel of
the ungodly, nor standeth in the way of sinners, nor
sitteth in the seat of the scornful.
But his delight is in the law of the Lord; and in his law
doth he meditate day and night.
And he shall be like a tree planted by the rivers of
water, that bringeth forth his fruit in his season; his
leaf also shall not wither; and whatsoever he doeth
shall prosper.
The ungodly are not so: but are like the chaff which
the wind driveth away. 1:1–4

Why do the heathen rage, and the people imagine a
vain thing? 2:1

Blessed are all they that put their trust in him. 2:12

Lord, lift thou up the light of thy countenance
upon us. 4:6

I will both lay me down in peace, and sleep. 4:8

Out of the mouth of babes and sucklings hast thou
ordained strength, because of thine enemies; that thou
mightest still the enemy and the avenger.
When I consider thy heavens, the work of thy fingers,
the moon and the stars, which thou hast ordained;
What is man, that thou art mindful of him? and the
son of man, that thou visitest him?
For thou hast made him a little lower than the angels.

8:2—5

How excellent is thy name in all the earth. 8:9

Flee as a bird to your mountain. 11:1

How long wilt thou forget me, O Lord? 13:1

The fool hath said in his heart, There is
no God. 11:1 and 53:1

Lord, who shall abide in thy tabernacle? who shall
dwell in thy holy hill? 15:1

He that sweareth to his own hurt, and
changeth not. 15:4

The lines are fallen unto me in pleasant places; yea, I
have a goodly heritage. 16:6

Keep me as the apple of the eye, hide me under the
shadow of thy wings. 17:8

He rode upon a cherub, and did fly: yea, he did fly
upon the wings of the wind. 18:10

The heavens declare the glory of God; and the
firmament showeth his handiwork.
Day unto day uttereth speech, and night unto night
showeth knowledge. 19:1–2

Their line is gone out through all the earth, and their
words to the end of the world. In them hath he set a
tabernacle for the sun,
Which is as a bridegroom coming out of his chamber,
and rejoiceth as a strong man to run a race.
His going forth is from the end of the heaven, and his
circuit unto the ends of it: and there is nothing hid
from the heat thereof. 19:4–6

The judgments of the Lord are true and righteous
altogether.
More to be desired are they than gold, yea, than
much fine gold: sweeter also than honey and the
honeycomb. *19:9–10*

Cleanse thou me from secret faults. *19:12*

Let the words of my mouth, and the meditation of my
heart, be acceptable in thy sight, O Lord, my
strength, and my redeemer. *19:14*

Thou hast given him his heart's desire. *21:2*

My God, my God, why hast thou forsaken me? why
art thou so far from helping me, and from the words
of my roaring? *22:1*

They part my garments among them, and cast lots
upon my vesture. *22:18*

The Lord is my shepherd; I shall not want.
He maketh me to lie down in green pastures: he
leadeth me beside the still waters.
He restoreth my soul: he leadeth me in the paths of
righteousness for his name's sake.

Yea, though I walk through the valley of the shadow
of death, I will fear no evil: for thou art with me; thy
rod and thy staff they comfort me.
Thou preparest a table before me in the presence of
mine enemies: thou anointest my head with oil; my
cup runneth over.
Surely goodness and mercy shall follow me all the
days of my life: and I will dwell in the house of the
Lord for ever. 23

The earth is the Lord's, and the fullness thereof; the
world, and they that dwell therein.
For he hath founded it upon the seas, and established
it upon the floods.
Who shall ascend into the hill of the Lord? or who
shall stand in his holy place?
He that hath clean hands, and a pure heart; who hath
not lifted up his soul unto vanity, nor sworn
deceitfully. 24:1–4

Lift up your heads, O ye gates; and be ye lift up, ye
everlasting doors; and the King of glory shall come in.

24:7

Who is this King of glory? The Lord of hosts, he is
the King of glory. 24:10

The Lord is my light and my salvation; whom shall I fear? the Lord is the strength of my life; of whom shall I be afraid? 27:1

Though an host should encamp against me, my heart shall not fear: though war should rise against me, in this will I be confident. 27:3

The Lord is my strength and my shield. 28:7

Worship the Lord in the beauty of holiness. 29:2

Weeping may endure for a night, but joy cometh in the morning. 30:5

I am forgotten as a dead man out of mind: I am like a broken vessel. 31:12

My times are in thy hand. 31:15

From the strife of tongues. 31:20

Sing unto him a new song; play skillfully with a loud noise. 33:3

O taste and see that the Lord is good. 34:8

Keep thy tongue from evil, and thy lips from speaking
guile.
Depart from evil, and do good; seek peace, and pursue
it. 34:13–14

Rescue my soul from their destructions, my darling
from the lions. 35:17

How excellent is thy lovingkindness, O God! 36:7

The meek shall inherit the earth. 37:11

I have been young, and now am old; yet have I not
seen the righteous forsaken, nor his seed begging
bread. 37:25

I have seen the wicked in great power, and spreading
himself like a green bay tree. 37:35

Mark the perfect man, and behold the upright: for the
end of that man is peace. 37:37

For thine arrows stick fast in me, and thy hand
presseth me sore. 38:2

I said, I will take heed to my ways, that I sin not with
my tongue. 39:1

My heart was hot within me, while I was musing the
fire burned. 39:3

Lord, make me to know mine end, and the measure of
my days, what it is; that I may know how frail I am.
39:4

Every man at his best state is altogether vanity. 39:5

Surely every man walketh in a vain show: surely they
are disquieted in vain: he heapeth up riches, and
knoweth not who shall gather them. 39:6

For I am a stranger with thee, and a sojourner, as all
my fathers were.
O spare me, that I may recover strength, before I go
hence, and be no more. 39:12–13

As the hart panteth after the water brooks, so panteth
my soul after thee, O God.
My soul thirsteth for God, for the living God. *42:1–2*

Why art thou cast down, O my soul? and why art
thou disquieted in me? *42:5*

Deep calleth unto deep. *42:7*

My tongue is the pen of a ready writer. *45:1*

The king's daughter is all glorious within. *45:13*

God is our refuge and strength, a very present help in
trouble.
Therefore will we not fear, though the earth be
removed, and though the mountains be carried into
the midst of the sea. *46:1–2*

There is a river, the streams whereof shall make glad
the city of God, the holy place of the tabernacles of
the most High.
God is in the midst of her; she shall not be moved:
God shall help her, and that right early. *46:4–5*

Be still, and know that I am God. *46:10*

Every beast of the forest is mine, and the cattle upon a
thousand hills. *50:10*

I was shapen in iniquity; and in sin did my mother
conceive me. *51:5*

Purge me with hyssop, and I shall be clean: wash me,
and I shall be whiter than snow. *51:7*

Create in me a clean heart, O God; and renew a right
spirit within me. *51:10*

And take not thy holy spirit from me. *51:11*

Open thou my lips; and my mouth shall show forth
thy praise. *51:15*

A broken and a contrite heart, O God, thou wilt not
despise. *51:17*

Oh that I had wings like a dove! for then would I fly
away, and be at rest. *55:6*

We took sweet counsel together. *55:14*

The words of his mouth were smoother than butter,
but war was in his heart: his words were softer than
oil, yet were they drawn swords. *55:21*

They are like the deaf adder that stoppeth her ear;
Which will not hearken to the voice of charmers,
charming never so wisely. *58:4–5*

Thou hast showed thy people hard things: thou hast
made us to drink the wine of astonishment. *60:3*

Moab is my washpot; over Edom will I cast out my
shoe: Philistia, triumph thou because of me. *60:8*

Lead me to the rock that is higher than I. *61:2*

He only is my rock and my salvation: he is my
defense; I shall not be moved. *62:6*

Thou renderest to every man according to his work.

62:12

My soul thirsteth for thee, my flesh longeth for thee
in a dry and thirsty land, where no water is. 63:1

Thou crownest the year with thy goodness. 65:11

Make a joyful noise unto God, all ye lands. 66:1

We went through fire and through water. 66:12

God setteth the solitary in families. 68:6

Cast me not off in the time of old age; forsake me not
when my strength faileth. 71:9

He shall come down like rain upon the mown grass: as
showers that water the earth. 72:6

His enemies shall lick the dust. 72:9

His name shall endure for ever. 72:17

A stubborn and rebellious generation. 78:8

Man did eat angels' food. 78:25

But ye shall die like men, and fall like one of the
princes. 82:7

How amiable are thy tabernacles, O Lord of hosts!
84:1

They go from strength to strength. 84:7

A day in thy courts is better than a thousand. I had
rather be a doorkeeper in the house of my God, than
to dwell in the tents of wickedness. 84:10

Mercy and truth are met together; righteousness and
peace have kissed each other. 85:10

Lord, why castest thou off my soul? why hidest thou
thy face from me? 88:14

Lord, thou hast been our dwelling place in all
generations.
Before the mountains were brought forth, or ever thou
hadst formed the earth and the world, even from
everlasting to everlasting, thou art God.
Thou turnest man to destruction; and sayest, Return,
ye children of men.

For the Lord is good; his mercy is everlasting; and his
truth endureth to all generations. *100*

My days are consumed like smoke. *102:3*

I watch, and am as a sparrow alone upon the
house top. *102:7*

As the heaven is high above the earth, so great is his
mercy toward them that fear him. *103:11*

As for man, his days are as grass: as a flower of the
field, so he flourisheth.
For the wind passeth over it, and it is gone; and the
place thereof shall know it no more *103:15—16*

Who layeth the beams of his chambers in the waters:
who maketh the clouds his chariot: who walketh upon
the wings of the wind. *104:3*

Wine that maketh glad the heart of man. *104:15*

The cedars of Lebanon. *104:16*

For a thousand years in thy sight are
when it is past, and as a watch
Thou carriest them away as with a
sleep: in the morning they are
groweth up
In the morning it flourisheth, a
evening it is cut down, an

We spend our years as

The days of our years a
and if by reason of stre
yet is their strength lab
off, and

So teach us to nur
our he

Establish thou t'
work of

He that dw
shall a
I will

ful

H g,
win

Th ove

Nor he

f rmed
A thou
thy rigl kneel

He shall of his
4–7

They sha

Thou shall 6:1
lion and t
ce. 97:1

The righteous ye lands.
before his
grow

he that l
Mightier this peop

g, and
im, a

He appointed the moon for seasons: the sun knoweth
his going down.
Thou makest darkness, and it is night: wherein all the
beasts of the forest do creep forth.
The young lions roar after their prey, and seek their
meat from God.
The sun ariseth, they gather themselves together, and
lay them down in their dens.
Man goeth forth unto his work and to his labor until
the evening.
O Lord, how manifold are thy works! in wisdom hast
thou made them all: the earth is full of thy riches.
So is this great and wide sea, wherein are things
creeping innumerable, both small and great beasts.
There go the ships: there is that leviathan, whom thou
hast made to play therein.
These wait all upon thee; that thou mayest give them
their meat in due season. *104:19–27*

The people asked, and he brought quails, and satisfied
them with the bread of heaven. *105:40*

Such as sit in darkness and in the shadow of death.
107:10

They that go down to the sea in ships, that do
business in great waters. *107:23*

They mount up to the heaven, they go down again to
the depths. *107:26*

They reel to and fro, and stagger like a drunken man,
and are at their wit's end. *107:27*

For I am poor and needy, and my heart is wounded
within me.
I am gone like the shadow when it declineth: I am
tossed up and down as the locust. *109:22–23*

Thou hast the dew of thy youth. *110:3*

The fear of the Lord is the beginning of wisdom.
111:10

From the rising of the sun unto the going down of the
same the Lord's name is to be praised. *113:3*

The mountains skipped like rams, and the little hills
like lambs. *114:4*

They have mouths, but they speak not: eyes have
they, but they see not.
They have ears, but they hear not. *115:5–6*

I said in my haste, All men are liars. *116:11*

Precious in the sight of the Lord is the death of his
saints. *116:15*

The stone which the builders refused is become the
head stone of the corner. *118:22*

This is the day which the Lord hath made. *118:24*

Blessed be he that cometh in the name of the Lord.
118:26

Thy word is a lamp unto my feet, and a light unto my
path. *119:105*

I am for peace: but when I speak, they are for war.
120:7

I will lift up mine eyes unto the hills, from whence
cometh my help.
My help cometh from the Lord, which made heaven
and earth.
He will not suffer thy foot to be moved: he that
keepeth thee will not slumber.

Behold, he that keepeth Israel shall neither slumber
nor sleep.
The Lord is thy keeper: the Lord is thy shade upon
thy right hand.
The sun shall not smite thee by day, nor the moon by
night.
The Lord shall preserve thee from all evil: he shall
preserve thy soul.
The Lord shall preserve thy going out and thy coming
in from this time forth, and even for evermore. *121*

I was glad when they said unto me, Let us go into the
house of the Lord. *122:1*

Peace be within thy walls, and prosperity within thy
palaces. *122:7*

They that sow in tears shall reap in joy.
He that goeth forth and weepeth, bearing precious
seed, shall doubtless come again with rejoicing,
bringing his sheaves with him. *126:5–6*

Except the Lord build the house, they labor in vain
that build it: except the Lord keep the city, the
watchman waketh but in vain. *127:1*

He giveth his beloved sleep. 127:2

As arrows are in the hand of a mighty man; so are
children of the youth.
Happy is the man that hath his quiver full of them.
127:4—5

Out of the depths have I cried unto thee, O Lord.
130:1

My soul waiteth for the Lord more than they that
watch for the morning. 130:6

I will not give sleep to mine eyes, or slumber to mine
eyelids. 132:4

Behold, how good and how pleasant it is for brethren
to dwell together in unity! 133:1

By the rivers of Babylon, there we sat down, yea, we
wept, when we remembered Zion.
We hanged our harps upon the willows in the midst
thereof
For there they that carried us away captive required of
us a song; and they that wasted us required of us
mirth, saying, Sing us one of the songs of Zion.

How shall we sing the Lord's song in a strange land?
If I forget thee, O Jerusalem, let my right hand forget
her cunning.
If I do not remember thee, let my tongue cleave to the
roof of my mouth.   *137:1–6*

O Lord, thou hast searched me, and known me.
Thou knowest my downsitting and mine uprising;
thou understandest my thought afar off.   *139:1–2*

Whither shall I go from thy Spirit? or whither shall I
flee from thy presence?
If I ascend up into heaven, thou art there: if I make my
bed in hell, behold, thou art there.
If I take the wings of the morning, and dwell in the
uttermost parts of the sea;
Even there shall thy hand lead me, and thy right hand
shall hold me.   *139:7–10*

The darkness and the light are both alike to thee.
139:12

I am fearfully and wonderfully made.   *139:14*

They have sharpened their tongues like
a serpent.   *140:3*

Thou openest thine hand, and satisfiest the desire of
every living thing. *145:16*

The Lord is nigh unto all them that call upon him, to
all that call upon him in truth. *145:18*

Put not your trust in princes. *146:3*

He telleth the number of the stars; he calleth them all
by their names. *147.4*

Praise him with the sound of the trumpet: praise him
with the psaltery and harp.
Praise him with the timbrel and dance: praise him
with stringed instruments and organs.
Praise him upon the loud cymbals: praise him upon
the high sounding cymbals.
Let every thing that hath breath praise the Lord.

150:3—6

THE PROVERBS

To give subtilty to the simple, to the young man
knowledge and discretion. *1:4*

My son, if sinners entice thee, consent thou not. *1:10*

Wisdom crieth without; she uttereth her voice in the
streets. *1:20*

Length of days is in her right hand; and in her left
hand riches and honor. *3:16*

Her ways are ways of pleasantness, and all her paths
are peace. *3:17*

Be not afraid of sudden fear. *3:25*

Wisdom is the principal thing; therefore get wisdom:
and with all thy getting get understanding. *4:7*

The path of the just is as the shining light, that
shineth more and more unto the perfect day. *4:18*

Keep thy heart with all diligence; for out of it are the
issues of life. *4:23*

The lips of a strange woman drop as a honeycomb,
and her mouth is smoother than oil:
But her end is bitter as wormwood, sharp as a two-
edged sword. *5:3–4*

Go to the ant, thou sluggard; consider her ways, and
be wise:
Which having no guide, overseer, or ruler,
Provideth her meat in the summer, and gathereth her
food in the harvest. *6:6–8*

Yet a little sleep, a little slumber, a little folding of the
hands to sleep:
So shall thy poverty come as one that traveleth, and
thy want as an armed man. *6:10–11*

Lust not after her beauty in thine heart; neither let her
take thee with her eyelids. *6:25*

Can a man take fire in his bosom, and his clothes not
be burned?
Can one go upon hot coals, and his feet not be
burned? *6:27–28*

Jealousy is the rage of a man: therefore he will not
spare in the day of vengeance. *6:34*

He goeth after her straightway, as an ox goeth to the
slaughter. 7:22

I love them that love me; and those that seek me early
shall find me. 8:17

Wisdom hath builded her house, she hath hewn out
her seven pillars. 9:1

Reprove not a scorner, lest he hate thee: rebuke a wise
man, and he will love thee. 9:8

Stolen waters are sweet, and bread eaten in secret is
pleasant. 9:17

A wise son maketh a glad father: but a foolish son is
the heaviness of his mother. 10:1

Blessings are upon the head of the just: but violence
covereth the mouth of the wicked.
The memory of the just is blessed: but the name of
the wicked shall rot. 10:6–7

Hatred stirreth up strifes: but love covereth all sins.
10:12

In the multitude of counsellors there is safety.
He that is surety for a stranger shall
smart for it. *11:14–15*

As a jewel of gold in a swine's snout, so is a fair
woman which is without discretion. *11:22*

He that trusteth in his riches shall fall. *11:28*

He that troubleth his own house shall inherit the
wind. *11:29*

A virtuous woman is a crown to her husband. *12:4*

A righteous man regardeth the life of his beast: but
the tender mercies of the wicked are cruel. *12:10*

The way of a fool is right in his own eyes *12:15*

Hope deferred maketh the heart sick. *13:12*

The way of transgressors is hard. *13:15*

The desire accomplished is sweet to the soul. *13:19*

He that spareth his rod hateth his son: but he that
loveth him chasteneth him betimes. *13:24*

Fools make a mock at sin. *14:9*

The heart knoweth his own bitterness; and a stranger
doth not intermeddle with his joy. *14:10*

Even in laughter the heart is sorrowful. *14:13*

The prudent man looketh well to his going. *14:15*

In all labor there is profit: but the talk of the lips
tendeth only to penury. *14:23*

Righteousness exalteth a nation. *14:34*

A soft answer turneth away wrath. *15:1*

A merry heart maketh a cheerful countenance: but by
sorrow of the heart the spirit is broken. *15:13*

He that is of a merry heart hath a continual feast.
Better is little with the fear of the Lord, than great
treasure, and trouble therewith.
Better is a dinner of herbs where love is, than a stalled
ox and hatred therewith. *15:15–17*

A wrathful man stirreth up strife: but he that is slow to
anger appeaseth strife. *15:18*

A word spoken in due season, how good is it! *15:23*

Before honor is humility. *15:33 and 18:12*

A man's heart deviseth his way: but the Lord directeth
his steps. *16:9*

Pride goeth before destruction, and an haughty spirit
before a fall. *16:18*

The hoary head is a crown of glory, if it be found in
the way of righteousness.
He that is slow to anger is better than the mighty; and
he that ruleth his spirit than he that taketh a city.

16:31–32

Whoso mocketh the poor reproacheth his Maker. *17:5*

He that repeateth a matter separateth very friends.
17:9

Whoso rewardeth evil for good, evil shall not depart
from his house. *17:13*

A merry heart doeth good like a medicine. *17:22*

He that hath knowledge spareth his words: and a man
of understanding is of an excellent spirit.
Even a fool, when he holdeth his peace, is counted
wise. *17:27–28*

A fool's mouth is his destruction. *18:7*

A wounded spirit who can bear? *18:14*

A brother offended is harder to be won than a strong
city: and their contentions are like the bars of a castle.
18:19

Whoso findeth a wife findeth a good thing. *18:22*

A man that hath friends must show himself friendly:
and there is a friend that sticketh closer than a
brother. 18:24

Wealth maketh many friends. 19:4

A foolish son is the calamity of his father: and the
contentions of a wife are a continual dropping. 19:13

He that hath pity upon the poor lendeth unto the
Lord. 19:17

Wine is a mocker, strong drink is raging 20:1

It is an honor for a man to cease from strife: but every
fool will be meddling. 20:3

Even a child is known by his doings, whether his work
be pure, and whether it be right.
The hearing ear, and the seeing eye, the Lord hath
made even both of them. 20:11–12

It is naught, it is naught, saith the buyer: but when he
is gone his way, then he boasteth. 20:14

Bread of deceit is sweet to a man; but afterwards his
mouth shall be filled with gravel. *20:17*

Meddle not with him that flattereth with his lips. *20:19*

It is better to dwell in a corner of the housetop, than
with a brawling woman in a wide house. *21:9 and 25:24*

A good name is rather to be chosen than great riches.

22:1

Train up a child in the way he should go; and when he
is old, he will not depart from it. *22:6*

The borrower is servant to the lender. *22:7*

Bow down thine ear, and hear the words of the wise,
and apply thine heart unto my knowledge.
For it is a pleasant thing if thou keep them within
thee; they shall withal be fitted in thy lips. *22:17–18*

Have I not written to thee excellent things in counsels
and knowledge,
That I might make thee know the certainty of the
words of truth; that thou mightest answer the words
of truth to them that send unto thee? 22:20–21

Rob not the poor, because he is poor: neither oppress
the afflicted in the gate. 22:22

Remove not the ancient landmark. 22:28

Seest thou a man diligent in his business? He shall
stand before kings. 22:29

Put a knife to thy throat, if thou be a man given to
appetite. 23:2

Labor not to be rich: cease from thine own wisdom.
23:4

Riches certainly make themselves wings; they fly away
as an eagle toward heaven. 23:5

As he thinketh in his heart, so is he. 23:7

The drunkard and the glutton shall come to poverty:
and drowsiness shall clothe a man with rags. 23:21

Despise not thy mother when she is old. 23:22

Look not thou upon the wine when it is red, when it
giveth his color in the cup, when it moveth itself
aright.
At the last it biteth like a serpent, and stingeth like an
adder. 23:31–32

A wise man is strong; yea, a man of knowledge
increaseth strength. 24:5

If thou faint in the day of adversity, thy strength is
small. 24:10

A word fitly spoken is like apples of gold in pictures of
silver. 25:11

If thine enemy be hungry, give him bread to eat; and
if he be thirsty, give him water to drink:
For thou shalt heap coals of fire upon
his head. 25:21–22

As cold waters to a thirsty soul, so is good news from
a far country. 25:25

For men to search their own glory is not glory. 25:27

Answer a fool according to his folly. 26:5

As a dog returneth to his vomit, so a fool returneth to
his folly.
Seest thou a man wise in his own conceit? There is
more hope of a fool than of him.
The slothful man saith, There is a lion in the way; a
lion is in the streets. 26:11–13

Whoso diggeth a pit shall fall therein: and he that
rolleth a stone, it will return upon him. 26:27

Boast not thyself of tomorrow, for thou knowest not
what a day may bring forth. 27:1

Let another man praise thee, and not thine own
mouth. 27:2

Open rebuke is better than secret love.
Faithful are the wounds of a friend; but the kisses of
an enemy are deceitful. 27:5–6

To the hungry soul every bitter thing is sweet. 27:7

Better is a neighbor that is near than a brother far off.
27:10

Iron sharpeneth iron; so a man sharpeneth the
countenance of his friend. 27:17

The wicked flee when no man pursueth: but the righteous are bold as a lion. 28:1

He that maketh haste to be rich shall not be innocent.
28:20

He that trusteth in his own heart is a fool. 28:26

He that giveth unto the poor shall not lack. 28:27

A fool uttereth all his mind. 29:11

Where there is no vision, the people perish. 29:18

A man's pride shall bring him low: but honor shall
uphold the humble in spirit. 29:23

Give me neither poverty nor riches. 30:8

Accuse not a servant unto his master. 30:10

The horseleach hath two daughters, crying, Give,
give. 30:15

There be three things which are too wonderful for
me, yea, four which I know not·
The way of an eagle in the air; the way of a serpent
upon a rock; the way of a ship in the midst of the sea;
and the way of a man with a maid. 30:18–19

Give strong drink unto him that is ready to perish,
and wine unto those that be of heavy hearts.
Let him drink, and forget his poverty, and remember
his misery no more. 31:6–7

Who can find a virtuous woman? for her price is far
above rubies.
The heart of her husband doth safely trust in her.

31:10–11

Her husband is known in the gates, when he sitteth
among the elders of the land. *31:23*

Strength and honor are her clothing. *31:25*

In her tongue is the law of kindness.
She looketh well to the ways of her household, and
eateth not the bread of idleness.
Her children arise up, and call her blessed. *31:26–28*

Many daughters have done virtuously, but thou
excellest them all.
Favor is deceitful, and beauty is vain: but a woman
that feareth the Lord, she shall be praised.
Give her of the fruit of her hands; and let her own
works praise her in the gates. *31:29–31*

ECCLESIASTES; OR, THE PREACHER

Vanity of vanities, saith the Preacher, vanity of
vanities; all is vanity.
What profit hath a man of all his labor which he
taketh under the sun?
One generation passeth away, and another generation
cometh: but the earth abideth for ever.
The sun also ariseth. *1:2–5*

All the rivers run into the sea; yet the sea is not full.
1:7

The eye is not satisfied with seeing, nor the ear filled
with hearing. *1:8*

The thing that hath been, it is that which shall be;
and that which is done is that which shall be done:
and there is no new thing under the sun. *1:9*

There is no remembrance of former things; neither
shall there be any remembrance of things that are to
come with those that shall come after. *1:11*

I have seen all the works that are done under the sun;
and, behold, all is vanity and vexation of spirit.
That which is crooked cannot be made straight: and
that which is wanting cannot be numbered. *1:14–15*

In much wisdom is much grief: and he that increaseth
knowledge increaseth sorrow. *1:18*

Wisdom excelleth folly, as far as light excelleth
darkness. *2:13*

One event happeneth to them all. *2:14*

How dieth the wise man? as the fool. *2:16*

To every thing there is a season, and a time to every
purpose under the heaven.
A time to be born, and a time to die; a time to plant,
and a time to pluck up that which is planted;
A time to kill, and a time to heal; a time to break
down, and a time to build up;
A time to weep, and a time to laugh; a time to mourn,
and a time to dance;
A time to cast away stones, and a time to gather
stones together; a time to embrace, and a time to
refrain from embracing;

A time to get, and a time to lose; a time to keep, and a
time to cast away;
A time to rend, and a time to sew; a time to keep
silence, and a time to speak;
A time to love, and a time to hate; a time of war, and a
time of peace. 3:1–8

Wherefore I praised the dead which are already dead
more than the living which are yet alive. 4:2

Better is a handful with quietness, than both the hands
full with travail and vexation of spirit. 4:6

A threefold cord is not quickly broken. 4:12

Better is a poor and a wise child than an old and
foolish king. 4:13

God is in heaven, and thou upon earth: therefore let
thy words be few. 5:2

Better is it that thou shouldest not vow, than that thou
shouldest vow and not pay. 5:5

The sleep of a laboring man is sweet . . . but the
abundance of the rich will not suffer him to sleep. 5:12

As he came forth of his mother's womb, naked shall he
return to go as he came, and shall take nothing of his
labor, which he may carry away in his hand. 5:15

A good name is better than precious ointment; and
the day of death than the day of one's birth. 7:1

It is better to go to the house of mourning, than to go
to the house of feasting. 7:2

The heart of the wise is in the house of mourning; but
the heart of fools is in the house of mirth. 7:4

As the crackling of thorns under a pot, so is the
laughter of the fool. 7:6

Better is the end of a thing than the beginning
thereof. 7:8

In the day of prosperity be joyful, but in the day of
adversity consider. 7:14

Be not righteous over much. 7:16

There is not a just man upon earth, that doeth good,
and sinneth not. 7:20

And I find more bitter than death the woman, whose
heart is snares and nets, and her hands as bands. 7:26

One man among a thousand have I found; but a
woman among all those have I not found. 7:28

God hath made man upright, but they have sought
out many inventions. 7:29

There is no discharge in that war. 8:8

A man hath no better thing under the sun, than to eat,
and to drink, and to be merry 8:15

A living dog is better than a dead lion.
For the living know that they shall die: but the dead
know not any thing, neither have they any more a
reward, for the memory of them is forgotten. 9:4–5

Whatsoever thy hand findeth to do, do it with thy
might; for there is no work, nor device, nor
knowledge, nor wisdom, in the grave, whither thou
goest. *9:10*

I returned, and saw under the sun, that the race is not
to the swift, nor the battle to the strong, neither yet
bread to the wise, nor yet riches to men of
understanding, nor yet favor to men of skill; but time
and chance happeneth to them all.
For man also knoweth not his time: as the fishes that
are taken in an evil net, and as the birds that are caught
in the snare; so are the sons of men snared in an evil
time, when it falleth suddenly upon them. *9:11–12*

A feast is made for laughter, and wine maketh merry:
but money answereth all things. *10:19*

A bird of the air shall carry the voice, and that which
hath wings shall tell the matter. *10:20*

Cast thy bread upon the waters: for thou shalt find it
after many days. *11:1*

He that observeth the wind shall not sow; and he that
regardeth the clouds shall not reap. *11:4*

Learn to do well; seek judgment, relieve the
oppressed, judge the fatherless, plead for the widow.
Come now, and let us reason together . . . though
your sins be as scarlet, they shall be as white as snow.

1:17—18

They shall beat their swords into plowshares, and
their spears into pruninghooks: nation shall not lift up
sword against nation, neither shall they learn war any
more. *2:4*

In that day a man shall cast his idols . . . to the moles
and to the bats. *2:20*

Cease ye from man, whose breath is in his nostrils.

2:22

The stay and the staff, the whole stay of bread, and
the whole stay of water. *3:1*

What mean ye that ye beat my people to pieces and
grind the faces of the poor? *3:15*

Walk with stretched forth necks and wanton eyes,
walking and mincing as they go, and making a
tinkling with their feet. *3:16*

In the morning sow thy seed, and in the evening
withhold not thine hand. *11:6*

Rejoice, O young man, in thy youth. *11:9*

Remember now thy Creator in the days of thy youth,
while the evil days come not, nor the years draw nigh,
when thou shalt say, I have no pleasure in them;
While the sun, or the light, or the moon, or the stars,
be not darkened, nor the clouds return after the rain:
In the day when the keepers of the house shall
tremble, and the strong men shall bow themselves,
and the grinders cease because they are few, and those
that look out of the windows be darkened,
And the doors shall be shut in the streets, when the
sound of the grinding is low, and he shall rise up at
the voice of the bird, and all the daughters of music
shall be brought low. *12:1–4*

The almond tree shall flourish, and the grasshop
shall be a burden, and desire shall fail; because
goeth to his long home, and the mourners go
the streets:
Or ever the silver cord be loosed, or the gold
be broken, or the pitcher be broken at the f
the wheel broken at the cistern,
Then shall the dust return to the earth as
the spirit shall return unto God who g

In that day seven women shall take hold of one man.

4:1

My wellbeloved hath a vineyard in a very fruitful hill.

5:1

And he looked for judgment, but behold oppression;
for righteousness, but behold a cry.
Woe unto them that join house to house, that lay field
to field, till there be no place, that they may be placed
alone in the midst of the earth! 5:7–8

Woe unto them that rise up early in the morning, that
they may follow strong drink. 5:11

Woe unto them that draw iniquity with cords of
vanity, and sin as it were with a cart rope. 5:18

Woe unto them that call evil good, and good evil. 5.20

I saw also the Lord sitting upon a throne, high and
lifted up, and his train filled the temple.
Above it stood the seraphims: each one had six wings;
with twain he covered his face, and with twain he
covered his feet, and with twain he did fly. 6:1–2

Holy, holy, holy, is the Lord of hosts: the whole earth
is full of his glory. 6:3

Woe is me! for I am undone; because I am a man of
unclean lips, and I dwell in the midst of a people of
unclean lips: for mine eyes have seen the King, the
Lord of hosts. 6:5

I heard the voice of the Lord, saying, Whom shall I
send, and who will go for us? Then said I, Here am I;
send me. 6:8

Then said I, Lord, how long? 6:11

Behold, a virgin shall conceive, and bear a son, and
shall call his name Immanuel. 7:14

For a stone of stumbling and for a rock of offense. 8:14

The people that walked in darkness have seen a great
light: they that dwell in the land of the shadow of
death, upon them hath the light shined. 9:2

For unto us a child is born, unto us a son is given: and
the government shall be upon his shoulder: and his
name shall be called Wonderful, Counsellor, The
mighty God, The everlasting Father, The Prince of
Peace.
Of the increase of his government and peace there
shall be no end. 9:6–7

The ancient and honorable, he is the head. 9:15

And there shall come forth a rod out of the stem of
Jesse, and a Branch shall grow out of his roots:
And the Spirit of the Lord shall rest upon him, the
spirit of wisdom and understanding, the spirit of
counsel and might, the spirit of knowledge and of the
fear of the Lord. 11:1–2

The wolf also shall dwell with the lamb, and the
leopard shall lie down with the kid; and the calf and
the young lion and the fatling together; and a little
child shall lead them.
And the cow and the bear shall feed; their young ones
shall lie down together: and the lion shall eat straw
like the ox.
And the suckling child shall play on the hole of the
asp, and the weaned child shall put his hand on the
cockatrice' den.

They shall not hurt nor destroy in all my holy
mountain: for the earth shall be full of the knowledge
of the Lord, as the waters cover the sea. *11:6–9*

For the Lord JEHOVAH is my strength and my song;
he also is become my salvation. *12:2*

And I will punish the world for their evil, and the
wicked for their iniquity; and I will cause the
arrogancy of the proud to cease, and will lay low the
haughtiness of the terrible. *13:11*

How art thou fallen from heaven, O Lucifer, son of
the morning! *14:12*

Is this the man that made the earth to tremble, that
did shake kingdoms. *14:16*

The nations shall rush like the rushing of many
waters. *17:13*

And they shall fight every one against his brother. *19:2*

The burden of the desert of the sea. As whirlwinds in the south pass through; so it cometh from the desert, from a terrible land. 21:1

Babylon is fallen, is fallen; and all the graven images of her gods he hath broken unto the ground. 21:9

Watchman, what of the night? 21:11

Let us eat and drink; for tomorrow we shall die. 22:13

I will fasten him as a nail in a sure place. 22:23

Whose merchants are princes. 23:8

As with the maid, so with her mistress. 24:2

For thou hast been a strength to the poor, a strength to the needy in his distress. 25:4

A feast of fat things, a feast of wines on the lees. 25:6

He will swallow up death in victory; and the Lord God will wipe away tears from off all faces. 25:8

Open ye the gates, that the righteous nation which
keepeth the truth may enter in.
Thou wilt keep him in perfect peace, whose mind is
stayed on thee.   26:2–3

Awake and sing, ye that dwell in dust.   26:19

Hide thyself as it were for a little moment, until the
indignation be overpast.   26:20

Leviathan that crooked serpent . . . the dragon that is
in the sea.   27:1

For precept must be upon precept, precept upon
precept; line upon line, line upon line; here a little,
and there a little.   28:10

We have made a covenant with death, and with hell
are we at agreement.   28:15

It shall be a vexation only to understand the report.

28:19

They are drunken, but not with wine; they stagger,
but not with strong drink.   29:9

Their strength is to sit still.
Now go, write it before them in a table, and note it in
a book, that it may be for the time to come for ever
and ever. 30:7–8

The bread of adversity, and the water of affliction.
30:20

This is the way, walk ye in it. 30:21

Behold, a king shall reign in righteousness. 32:1

And a man shall be as an hiding place from the wind,
and a covert from the tempest; as rivers of water in a
dry place, as the shadows of a great rock in a weary
land. 32:2

An habitation of dragons, and a court for owls. 34:13

The desert shall rejoice, and blossom as the rose. 35:1

Then the eyes of the blind shall be opened, and the
ears of the deaf shall be unstopped.
Then shall the lame man leap as an hart, and the
tongue of the dumb sing. 35:5–6

Sorrow and sighing shall flee away. *35:10*

Thou trustest in the staff of this broken reed. *36:6*

Incline thine ear, O Lord, and hear. *37:17*

I shall go softly all my years in the bitterness of my
soul. *38:15*

Comfort ye, comfort ye my people. *40:1*

Speak ye comfortably to Jerusalem, and cry unto her,
that her warfare is accomplished, that her iniquity is
pardoned: for she hath received of the Lord's hand
double for all her sins.
The voice of him that crieth in the wilderness,
Prepare ye the way of the Lord, make straight in the
desert a highway for our God. *40:2–3*

Every valley shall be exalted, and every mountain and
hill shall be made low: and the crooked shall be made
straight, and the rough places plain. *40:4*

The voice said, Cry. And he said, what shall I cry? All flesh is grass, and all the goodliness thereof is as the flower of the field. *40:6*

The grass withereth, the flower fadeth; but the word of our God shall stand for ever. *40:8*

Get thee up into the high mountain . . . say unto the cities of Judah, Behold your God! *40:9*

He shall feed his flock like a shepherd: he shall gather the lambs with his arm, and carry them in his bosom, and shall gently lead those that are with young. *40:11*

The nations are as a drop of a bucket, and are counted as the small dust of the balance. *40:15*

Have ye not known? have ye not heard? hath it not been told you from the beginning? *40:21*

They that wait upon the Lord shall renew their strength; they shall mount up with wings as eagles; they shall run, and not be weary, and they shall walk, and not faint. *40:31*

They helped every one his neighbor; and every one
said to his brother, Be of good courage. *41:6*

A bruised reed shall he not break, and the smoking
flax shall he not quench. *42:3*

Shall the clay say to him that fashioneth it, What
makest thou? *45:9*

Behold, I have refined thee, but not with silver; I have
chosen thee in the furnace of affliction. *48:10*

O that thou hadst hearkened to my commandments!
then had thy peace been as a river, and thy righteousness as the waves of the sea. *48:18*

There is no peace, saith the Lord, unto the wicked.

48:22

Therefore the redeemed of the Lord shall return, and
come with singing unto Zion. *51:11*

Thou hast drunken the dregs of the cup of trembling.

51:17

Therefore hear now this.　51:21

How beautiful upon the mountains are the feet of him
that bringeth good tidings, that publisheth peace.　52:7

They shall see eye to eye.　52:8

He is despised and rejected of men; a man of sorrows,
and acquainted with grief.　53:3

Surely he hath borne our griefs, and carried our
sorrows.　53:4

All we like sheep have gone astray.　53:6

He is brought as a lamb to the slaughter.　53:7

Ho, everyone that thirsteth, come ye to the waters.
55:1

Behold, I have given him for a witness to the people, a
leader and commander to the people.　55:4

Let the wicked forsake his way, and the unrighteous
man his thoughts. *55:7*

For my thoughts are not your thoughts, neither are
your ways my ways, saith the Lord. *55:8*

Peace to him that is far off, and to him that is near.
57:19

Arise, shine; for thy light is come, and the glory of the
Lord is risen upon thee. *60:1*

A little one shall become a thousand, and a small one
a strong nation. *60:22*

Give unto them beauty for ashes, the oil of joy for
mourning, the garment of praise for the spirit of
heaviness. *61:3*

I have trodden the winepress alone; and of the people
there was none with me: for I will tread them in mine
anger, and trample them in my fury; and their blood
shall be sprinkled upon my garments, and I will stain
all my raiment. *63:3*

All our righteousnesses are as filthy rags; and we all do fade as a leaf. *64:6*

We all are the work of thy hand. *64:8*

I am holier than thou. *65:5*

For, behold, I create new heavens and a new earth. *65:17*

And they shall build houses, and inhabit them; and they shall plant vineyards, and eat the fruit of them. They shall not build, and another inhabit; they shall not plant, and another eat. *65:21–22*

As one whom his mother comforteth, so will I comfort you. *66:13*

THE BOOK OF THE PROPHET JEREMIAH

They were as fed horses in the morning: every one neighed after his neighbor's wife. *5:8*

Hear now this, O foolish people, and without understanding; which have eyes, and see not; which have ears, and hear not. *5:21*

But this people hath a revolting and a rebellious heart.

5:23

Saying, Peace, peace; when there is no peace.

6:14 and 8:11

Stand ye in the ways, and see, and ask for the old paths, where is the good way, and walk therein. *6:16*

Amend your ways and your doings. *7:3 and 26:13*

The harvest is past, the summer is ended, and we are not saved. *8:20*

Is there no balm in Gilead? *8:22*

Oh that I had in the wilderness a lodging place of wayfaring men! *9:2*

Thus saith the Lord, Let not the wise man glory in his wisdom, neither let the mighty man glory in his might, let not the rich man glory in his riches: But let him that glorieth glory in this, that he understandeth and knoweth me. 9:23–24

Can the Ethiopian change his skin, or the leopard his spots? 13:23

Our backslidings are many; we have sinned against thee. 14:7

Her sun is gone down while it was yet day 15·9

A man of strife and a man of contention. 15:10

The sin of Judah is written with a pen of iron, and with the point of a diamond. 17:1

Cursed be the man that trusteth in man, and maketh flesh his arm, and whose heart departeth from the Lord.
For he shall be like the heath in the desert, and shall not see when good cometh; but shall inhabit the parched places in the wilderness, in a salt land and not inhabited.

Blessed is the man that trusteth in the Lord, and
whose hope the Lord is.
For he shall be as a tree planted by the waters, and
that spreadeth out her roots by the river, and shall not
see when heat cometh, but her leaf shall be green; and
shall not be careful in the year of drought, neither
shall cease from yielding fruit. *17:5–8*

The heart is deceitful above all things, and desperately
wicked: who can know it? *17:9*

As the partridge sitteth on eggs, and hatcheth them
not; so he that getteth riches, and not by right, shall
leave them in the midst of his days, and at his end
shall be a fool. *17:11*

Thou art my hope in the day of evil. *17:17*

O earth, earth, earth, hear the word of the Lord. *22:29*

A curse, and an astonishment, and a hissing, and a
reproach. *29:18*

The fathers have eaten a sour grape, and the children's
teeth are set on edge. *31:29*

With my whole heart and with my whole soul. 32:41

And seekest thou great things for thyself? seek them
not. 45:5

THE LAMENTATIONS OF JEREMIAH

How doth the city sit solitary, that was full of people!
how is she become as a widow! 1:1

She weepeth sore in the night, and her tears are on
her cheeks: among all her lovers she hath none to
comfort her. 1:2

Is it nothing to you, all ye that pass by? behold, and
see if there be any sorrow like unto my sorrow. 1:12

Remembering mine affliction and my misery, the
wormwood and the gall. 3:19

It is good for a man that he bear the yoke in his
youth. 3:27

THE BOOK OF THE PROPHET EZEKIEL

As it were a wheel in the middle of a wheel. *1:16*

As is the mother, so is her daughter. *16:44*

The king of Babylon stood at the parting of the way.

21:21

The valley . . . was full of bones . . . and lo, they were
very dry. *37:1–2*

Can these bones live? *37:3*

O ye dry bones, hear the word of the Lord. *37:4*

Every man's sword shall be against his brother. *38:21*

THE BOOK OF DANIEL

His legs of iron, his feet part of iron and part of clay.

2:33

Shadrach, Meshach, and Abednego, fell down bound
into the midst of the burning fiery furnace. 3:23

Nebuchadnezzar . . . was driven from men, and did
eat grass as oxen. 4:33

Belshazzar the king made a great feast to a thousand
of his lords. 5:1

And this is the writing that was written, MENE,
MENE, TEKEL, UPHARSIN.
This is the interpretation of the thing: MENE; God
hath numbered thy kingdom, and finished it.
TEKEL; Thou art weighed in the balances, and art
found wanting.
PERES; Thy kingdom is divided, and given to the
Medes and Persians. 5:25–28

According to the law of the Medes and Persians,
which altereth not. 6:12

They brought Daniel, and cast him into the den of
lions. 6:16

So Daniel was taken up out of the den, and no manner of hurt was found upon him, because he believed in his God. *6:23*

The Ancient of days. *7:9 and 7:13*

Many shall run to and fro, and knowledge shall be increased. *12:4*

HOSEA

Ye are the sons of the living God. *1:10*

Like people, like priest. *4:9*

After two days will he revive us: in the third day he will raise us up, and we shall live in his sight. *6:2*

He shall come unto us as the rain, as the latter and former rain unto the earth. *6:3*

For I desired mercy, and not sacrifice; and the knowledge of God more than burnt offerings. *6:6*

They have sown the wind, and they shall reap the
whirlwind. 8:7

Ye have plowed wickedness, ye have reaped iniquity.
10:13

I drew them with . . . bands of love. 11:4

I have multiplied visions, and used similitudes, by the
ministry of the prophets. 12:10

I will ransom them from the power of the grave; I will
redeem them from death: O death, I will be thy
plagues; O grave, I will be thy destruction. 13:14

JOEL

Your old men shall dream dreams, your young men
shall see visions. 2:28

Multitudes in the valley of decision. 3:14

AMOS

They sold the righteous for silver, and the poor for a
pair of shoes. *2:6*

Can two walk together, except they be agreed? *3:3*

Woe to them that are at ease in Zion. *6:1*

JONAH

And Jonah was in the belly of the fish three days and
three nights. *1:17*

MICAH

What doth the Lord require of thee, but to do justly,
and to love mercy, and to walk humbly with thy God?

6:8

NAHUM

The faces of them all gather blackness. 2:10

HABAKKUK

Write the vision, and make it plain upon tables, that
he may run that readeth it. 2:2

The stone shall cry out of the wall, and the beam out
of the timber shall answer it. 2:11

The Lord is in his holy temple: let all the earth keep
silence before him. 2:20

ZECHARIAH

Your fathers, where are they? And the prophets, do
they live forever? 1:5

I have spread you abroad as the four winds of the
heaven. 2:6

Not by might, nor by power, but by my spirit, saith
the Lord of hosts. *4:6*

For who hath despised the day of small things? *4:10*

Behold, thy King cometh unto thee . . . lowly, and
riding upon an ass. *9:9*

Prisoners of hope. *9:12*

So they weighed for my price thirty pieces of silver.
11:12

What are these wounds in thine hands? . . . Those
with which I was wounded in the house of my friends.
13:6

MALACHI

Have we not all one father? hath not one God created
us? *2:10*

JUDITH

Put on her garments of gladness. 10:3

THE WISDOM OF SOLOMON

The ear of jealousy heareth all things. 1:10

Our time is a very shadow that passeth away. 2:5

Let us crown ourselves with rosebuds, before they be
withered. 2:8

For God created man to be immortal, and made him
to be an image of his own eternity.
Nevertheless through envy of the devil came death
into the world. 2:23–24

The souls of the righteous are in the hand of God, and
there shall no torment touch them.
In the sight of the unwise they seemed to die: and
their departure is taken for misery,
And their going from us to be utter destruction: but
they are in peace.

The Apocrypha

I ESDRAS

And when they are in their cups, they forget their
love both to friends and brethren, and a little after
draw out swords. 3:22

Great is Truth, and mighty above all things. 4:41

II ESDRAS

What is past I know, but what is for to come I know
not. 4:46

Now therefore keep thy sorrow to thyself, and bear
with a good courage that which hath befallen thee.
10:15

I shall light a candle of understanding in thine hear
which shall not be put out. 14:25

TOBIT

If thou hast abundance, give alms accordingly: i
have but a little, be not afraid to give accordir
that little. 4:8

For though they be punished in the sight of men, yet
is their hope full of immortality.
And having been a little chastised, they shall be
greatly rewarded: for God proved them, and found
them worthy for himself. *3:1–5*

They that put their trust in him shall understand the
truth. *3:9*

Even so we in like manner, as soon as we were born,
began to draw to our end. *5:13*

For the hope of the ungodly is like dust that is blown
away with the wind . . . and passeth away as the
remembrance of a guest that tarrieth but a day. *5:14*

For the very true beginning of her [wisdom] is the
desire of discipline; and the care of discipline is love.

6:17

And when I was born, I drew in the common air, and
fell upon the earth, which is of like nature; and the
first voice which I uttered was crying, as all others do.

7:3

All men have one entrance into life, and the like going
out. 7:6

.

The light that cometh from her [wisdom] never goeth
out. 7:10

THE WISDOM OF JESUS THE SON OF SIRACH, OR ECCLESIASTICUS

Who can number the sand of the sea, and the drops of
rain, and the days of eternity? 1:2

To whom hath the root of wisdom been revealed? 1:6

For the Lord is full of compassion and mercy, long-
suffering, and very pitiful, and forgiveth sins, and
saveth in time of affliction. 2:11

The greater thou art, the more humble thyself. 3:18

Many are in high place, and of renown: but mysteries
are revealed unto the meek. 3:19

Seek not out the things that are too hard for thee,
neither search the things that are above thy strength.

3:21

Be not curious in unnecessary matters: for more things
are showed unto thee than men understand.   3:23

Profess not the knowledge . . . that thou hast not.
A stubborn heart shall fare evil at the last.   3:25–26

Defraud not the poor of his living, and make not the
needy eyes to wait long.   4:1

Wisdom exalteth her children, and layeth hold of
them that seek her.
He that loveth her loveth life.   4:11–12

Observe the opportunity.   4:20

Be not as a lion in thy house, nor frantic among thy
servants.
Let not thine hand be stretched out to receive, and
shut when thou shouldest repay.   4:30–31

Set not thy heart upon thy goods; and say not, I have enough for my life. *5:1*

Winnow not with every wind, and go not into every way. *5:9*

Let thy life be sincere. *5:11*

Be not ignorant of any thing in a great matter or a small. *5:15*

If thou wouldest get a friend, prove him first. *6:7*

A faithful friend is a strong defense: and he that hath found such an one hath found a treasure. *6:14*

A faithful friend is the medicine of life. *6:16*

If thou seest a man of understanding, get thee betimes unto him, and let thy foot wear the steps of his door.

6:36

Whatsoever thou takest in hand, remember the end, and thou shalt never do amiss. *7:36*

Rejoice not over thy greatest enemy being dead, but remember that we die all. 8:7

Miss not the discourse of the elders. 8:9

Forsake not an old friend; for the new is not comparable to him: a new friend is as new wine; when it is old, thou shalt drink it with pleasure. 9:10

Pride is hateful before God and man. 10:7

He that is today a king tomorrow shall die. 10.10

Pride was not made for men, nor furious anger for them that are born of a woman. 10:18

Be not overwise in doing thy business. 10·26

Many kings have sat down upon the ground; and one that was never thought of hath worn the crown. 11:5

In the day of prosperity there is a forgetfulness of affliction: and in the day of affliction there is no more remembrance of prosperity. 11:25

Judge none blessed before his death. *11:28*

A friend cannot be known in prosperity: and an
enemy cannot be hidden in adversity. *12:8*

He that toucheth pitch shall be defiled therewith. *13:1*

How agree the kettle and the earthen pot together?
13:2

All flesh consorteth according to kind, and a man will
cleave to his like. *13:16*

A rich man beginning to fall is held up of his friends:
but a poor man being down is thrust also away by his
friends. *13:21*

The heart of a man changeth his countenance,
whether it be for good or evil. *13:25*

So is a word better than a gift. *18:16*

Be not made a beggar by banqueting upon borrowing.
18:33

He that contemneth small things shall fall by little and little. 19:1

Whether it be to friend or foe, talk not of other men's lives. 19:8

A man's attire, and excessive laughter, and gait, show what he is. 19:30

A tale out of season [is as] music in mourning. 22:6

I will not be ashamed to defend a friend. 22:25

All wickedness is but little to the wickedness of a woman. 25:19

The discourse of fools is irksome. 27:13

Many have fallen by the edge of the sword: but not so many as have fallen by the tongue. 28:18

Better is the life of a poor man in a mean cottage, than delicate fare in another man's house. 29:22

There is no riches above a sound body.   30:16

Gladness of the heart is the life of a man, and the
joyfulness of a man prolongeth his days.   30:22

Envy and wrath shorten the life, and carefulness
bringeth age before the time.   30:24

Watching for riches consumeth the flesh, and the care
thereof driveth away sleep.   31:1

Let thy speech be short, comprehending much in few
words.   32:8

Consider that I labored not for myself only, but for all
them that seek learning.   33:17

Leave not a stain in thine honor.   33:22

Let the counsel of thine own heart stand.   37:13

Honor a physician with the honor due unto him for
the uses which ye may have of him: for the Lord hath
created him.   38:1

When the dead is at rest, let his remembrance rest;
and be comforted for him, when his spirit is departed
from him. 38:23

How can he get wisdom . . . whose talk is of bullocks?
38:25

Let us now praise famous men, and our fathers that
begat us. 44:1

All these were honored in their generations, and were
the glory of their times.
There be of them, that have left a name behind them,
that their praises might be reported.
And some there be, which have no memorial; who are
perished, as though they had never been; and are
become as though they had never been born; and
their children after them 44:7–9

Their bodies are buried in peace; but their name liveth
for evermore. 44:14

His word burned like a lamp. 48:1

THE SONG OF THE THREE HOLY CHILDREN

O all ye works of the Lord, bless ye the Lord: praise
him and exalt him above all for ever. *35*

THE HISTORY OF SUSANNA

Daniel had convicted them of false witness by their
own mouth. *61*

THE SECOND BOOK OF THE MACCABEES

It is a foolish thing to make a long prologue, and to be
short in the story itself. *2:32*

When he was at the last gasp. *7:9*

Speech finely framed delighteth the ears. *15:39*

The New Testament

THE GOSPEL ACCORDING TO SAINT MATTHEW

Behold, a virgin shall be with child, and shall bring
forth a son, and they shall call his name Emmanuel,
which being interpreted is, God with us. 1:23

Now when Jesus was born in Bethlehem of Judaea in
the days of Herod the king, behold, there came wise
men from the east to Jerusalem,
Saying, Where is he that is born King of the Jews? for
we have seen his star in the east, and are come to
worship him. 2:1–2

They saw the young child with Mary his mother, and
fell down, and worshipped him: and . . . they
presented unto him gifts; gold, and frankincense, and
myrrh.
And being warned of God in a dream that they should
not return to Herod, they departed into their own
country another way. 2:11–12

Out of Egypt have I called my son. 2:15

Rachel weeping for her children, and would not be
comforted, because they are not. 2:18

He shall be called a Nazarene. 2:23

Repent ye: for the kingdom of heaven is at hand. 3:2

The voice of one crying in the wilderness, Prepare ye
the way of the Lord, make his paths straight. 3:3

And his meat was locusts and wild honey. 3:4

O generation of vipers, who hath warned you to flee
from the wrath to come? 3:7

Now also the axe is laid unto the root of the trees:
therefore every tree which bringeth not forth good
fruit is hewn down, and cast into the fire. 3:10

The Spirit of God descending like a dove. 3:16

This is my beloved Son, in whom I am well pleased.
3:17

And when he had fasted forty days and forty nights,
he was afterward an hungred. 4:2

The people which sat in darkness saw great light. 4:16

Follow me, and I will make you fishers of men. 4:19

Blessed are the poor in spirit: for theirs is the kingdom
of heaven.
Blessed are they that mourn: for they shall be
comforted.
Blessed are the meek: for they shall inherit the earth.
Blessed are they which do hunger and thirst after righ-
teousness: for they shall be filled.
Blessed are the merciful: for they shall obtain mercy.
Blessed are the pure in heart: for they shall see God.
Blessed are the peacemakers: for they shall be called
the children of God.
Blessed are they which are persecuted for righ-
teousness' sake: for theirs is the kingdom of heaven.
Blessed are ye, when men shall revile you, and
persecute you, and shall say all manner of evil against
you falsely, for my sake. 5:3 11

Ye are the salt of the earth: but if the salt have lost his
savor, wherewith shall it be salted? 5:13

Ye are the light of the world. A city that is set on an
hill cannot be hid.
Neither do men light a candle, and put it under a
bushel, but on a candlestick; and it giveth light unto
all that are in the house.
Let your light so shine before men, that they may see
your good works, and glorify your Father which is in
heaven.
Think not that I am come to destroy the law, or the
prophets: I am not come to destroy, but to fulfill. *5:14–17*

Till heaven and earth pass, one jot or one tittle shall in
no wise pass from the law, till all be fulfilled. *5:18*

Whosoever looketh on a woman to lust after her hath
committed adultery with her already in his heart.
And if thy right eye offend thee, pluck it out, and cast
it from thee: for it is profitable for thee that one of thy
members should perish, and not that thy whole body
should be cast into hell.
And if thy right hand offend thee, cut it off. *5:28–30*

Swear not at all; neither by heaven; for it is God's
throne:
Nor by the earth; for it is his footstool. *5:34–35*

Resist not evil: but whosoever shall smite thee on thy
right cheek, turn to him the other also. *5:39*

Love your enemies, bless them that curse you, do
good to them that hate you, and pray for them which
despitefully use you, and persecute you. *5:44*

He maketh his sun to rise on the evil and on the good,
and sendeth rain on the just and on the unjust. *5:45*

Be ye therefore perfect, even as your Father which is
in heaven is perfect. *5:48*

When thou doest alms, let not thy left hand know
what thy right hand doeth. *6:3*

After this manner therefore pray ye: Our Father which
art in heaven, Hallowed be thy name.
Thy kingdom come. Thy will be done in earth, as it is
in heaven
Give us this day our daily bread.
And forgive us our debts, as we forgive our debtors.
And lead us not into temptation, but deliver us from
evil: For thine is the kingdom, and the power, and the
glory, for ever. Amen. *6:9–13*

Lay not up for yourselves treasures upon earth, where
moth and rust doth corrupt, and where thieves break
through and steal:
But lay up for yourselves treasures in heaven.   6:19–20

For where your treasure is, there will your heart
be also.   6:21

The light of the body is the eye.   6:22

If therefore the light that is in thee be darkness, how
great is that darkness!   6:23

No man can serve two masters: for either he will hate
the one, and love the other; or else he will hold to the
one, and despise the other. Ye cannot serve God and
mammon.   6:24

Is not the life more than meat, and the body than
raiment?
Behold the fowls of the air: for they sow not, neither
do they reap, nor gather into barns.   6:25–26

Which of you by taking thought can add one cubit
unto his stature?   6:27

Consider the lilies of the field, how they grow; they toil not, neither do they spin. 6:28

Even Solomon in all his glory was not arrayed like one of these. 6:29

Seek ye first the kingdom of God, and his righteousness; and all these things shall be added unto you. 6:33

Take therefore no thought for the morrow: for the morrow shall take thought for the things of itself. Sufficient unto the day is the evil thereof. 6:34

Judge not, that ye be not judged. 7:1

With what measure ye mete, it shall be measured to you again.
And why beholdest thou the mote that is in thy brother's eye, but considerest not the beam that is in thine own eye? 7:2–3

Thou hypocrite, first cast out the beam out of thine own eye. 7:5

Neither cast ye your pearls before swine. *7:6*

Ask, and it shall be given you; seek, and ye shall find;
knock, and it shall be opened unto you. *7:7*

Or what man is there of you, whom if his son ask
bread, will he give him a stone? *7:9*

Therefore all things whatsoever ye would that men
should do to you, do ye even so to them: for this is
the law and the prophets. *7:12*

Wide is the gate, and broad is the way, that leadeth to
destruction, and many there be which go in thereat:
Because strait is the gate, and narrow is the way,
which leadeth unto life, and few there be that find it.

7:13–14

Beware of false prophets, which come to you in
sheep's clothing, but inwardly they are ravening
wolves. *7:15*

Ye shall know them by their fruits. Do men gather
grapes of thorns, or figs of thistles? *7:16*

By their fruits ye shall know them. 7:20

Not every one that saith unto me, Lord, Lord, shall enter into the kingdom of heaven; but he that doeth the will of my Father which is in heaven. 7:21

[The house] fell not: for it was founded upon a rock.
7:25

A foolish man, which built his house upon the sand.
7:26

But the children of the kingdom shall be cast out into outer darkness: there shall be weeping and gnashing of teeth. 8:12

The foxes have holes, and the birds of the air have nests; but the Son of man hath not where to lay his head. 8:20

Follow me; and let the dead bury their dead. 8:22

Why are ye fearful, O ye of little faith? 8:26

He saw a man, named Matthew, sitting at the receipt
of custom. *9:9*

They that be whole need not a physician, but they
that are sick. *9:12*

I am not come to call the righteous, but sinners to
repentance. *9:13*

Can the children of the bridechamber mourn, as long
as the bridegroom is with them? *9:15*

Neither do men put new wine into old bottles. *9:17*

The maid is not dead, but sleepeth. *9:24*

The harvest truly is plenteous, but the laborers
are few. *9:37*

Go rather to the lost sheep of the house of Israel. *10:6*

Freely ye have received, freely give. *10:8*

Whosoever shall not receive you, nor hear your
words, when ye depart out of that house or city, shake
off the dust of your feet. *10:14*

Be ye therefore wise as serpents, and harmless as
doves. *10:16*

Ye shall be hated of all men for my name's sake. *10:22*

The disciple is not above his master, nor the servant
above his lord. *10:24*

Are not two sparrows sold for a farthing? and one of
them shall not fall on the ground without your Father.
But the very hairs of your head are all numbered.

10:29–30

I came not to send peace, but a sword. *10:34*

He that taketh not his cross, and followeth after me, is
not worthy of me.
He that findeth his life shall lose it: and he that loseth
his life for my sake shall find it. *10:38–39*

He that hath ears to hear, let him hear. *11:15*

The Son of man came eating and drinking, and they
say, Behold a man gluttonous, and a winebibber, a
friend of publicans and sinners. But wisdom is justified
of her children. *11:19*

Come unto me, all ye that labor and are heavy laden,
and I will give you rest.
Take my yoke upon you, and learn of me; for I am
meek and lowly in heart: and ye shall find rest unto
your souls.
For my yoke is easy, and my burden is light. *11:28–30*

He that is not with me is against me. *12:30*

The tree is known by his fruit. *12:33*

Out of the abundance of the heart the mouth
speaketh. *12:34*

Behold, a greater than Solomon is here. *12:42*

Some seeds fell by the way side. *13:4*

Because they had no root, they withered away. *13.6*

But other fell into good ground, and brought forth fruit, some an hundredfold, some sixtyfold, some thirtyfold. 13:8

The care of this world, and the deceitfulness of riches.

13:22

The kingdom of heaven is like to a grain of mustard seed. 13:31

Pearl of great price. 13:46

The kingdom of heaven is like unto a net, that was cast into the sea, and gathered of every kind. 13:47

Is not this the carpenter's son? 13:55

A prophet is not without honor, save in his own country. 13:57

[Salome] the daughter of Herodias danced before them, and pleased Herod. 14:6

Give me here John Baptist's head in a charger. 14:8

We have here but five loaves, and two fishes. *14:17*

And they did all eat, and were filled: and they took up of the fragments that remained twelve baskets full.
14:20

And in the fourth watch of the night Jesus went unto them, walking on the sea. *14:25*

Be of good cheer; it is I; be not afraid. *14:27*

O thou of little faith, wherefore didst thou doubt?
14:31

Of a truth thou art the Son of God. *14:33*

Not that which goeth into the mouth defileth a man; but that which cometh out of the mouth, this defileth a man. *15:11*

They be blind leaders of the blind. And if the blind lead the blind, both shall fall into the ditch. *15:14*

The dogs eat of the crumbs which fall from their masters' table. *15:27*

When it is evening, ye say, It will be fair weather: for
the sky is red.   16:2

The signs of the times.   16:3

Thou art the Christ, the Son of the living God.   16:16

Thou art Peter, and upon this rock I will build my
church; and the gates of hell shall not prevail
against it.
And I will give unto thee the keys of the kingdom of
heaven.   16:18–19

Get thee behind me, Satan.   16:23

Whosoever will save his life shall lose it: and
whosoever will lose his life for my sake shall find it.
For what is a man profited, if he shall gain the whole
world, and lose his own soul?   16:25–26

Except ye be converted, and become as little children,
ye shall not enter into the kingdom of heaven.   18:3

He rejoiceth more of that sheep, than of the ninety
and nine which went not astray.   18:13

Where two or three are gathered together in my name, there am I in the midst of them. *18:20*

Until seventy times seven. *18:22*

What therefore God hath joined together, let not man put asunder. *19:6*

If thou wilt be perfect, go and sell that thou hast, and give to the poor, and thou shalt have treasure in heaven. *19:21*

It is easier for a camel to go through the eye of a needle, than for a rich man to enter into the kingdom of God. *19:24*

Many that are first shall be last; and the last shall be first. *19:30*

Borne the burden and heat of the day. *20:12*

Is it not lawful for me to do what I will with mine own? *20:15*

Overthrew the tables of the moneychangers. *21:12*

My house shall be called the house of prayer; but ye
have made it a den of thieves.   21:13

They made light of it.   22:5

Many are called, but few are chosen.   22:14

Render therefore unto Caesar the things which are
Caesar's; and unto God the things that are God's.   22:21

Thou shalt love the Lord thy God with all thy heart,
and with all thy soul, and with all thy mind.
This is the first and great commandment.
And the second is like unto it, Thou shalt love thy
neighbor as thyself.
On these two commandments hang all the law and
the prophets.   22:37–40

Whosoever shall exalt himself shall be abased; and he
that shall humble himself shall be exalted.   23:12

Woe unto you, scribes and Pharisees, hypocrites! for
ye pay tithe of mint and anise and cumin.   23:23

Blind guides, which strain at a gnat, and swallow a
camel. 23:24

Whited sepulchers, which indeed appear beautiful
outward, but are within full of dead men's bones. 23:27

O Jerusalem, Jerusalem, thou that killest the prophets,
and stonest them which are sent unto thee, how often
would I have gathered thy children together, even as a
hen gathereth her chickens under her wings, and ye
would not! 23:37

Ye shall hear of wars and rumors of wars: see that ye
be not troubled: for all these things must come to
pass, but the end is not yet.
For nation shall rise against nation. 24:6–7

Abomination of desolation. 24:15

Wheresoever the carcase is, there will the eagles be
gathered together. 24:28

And he shall send his angels with a great sound of a
trumpet. 24:31

Heaven and earth shall pass away, but my words shall
not pass away. 24:35

The one shall be taken, and the other left. 24:40

Then shall the kingdom of heaven be likened unto ten
virgins, which took their lamps, and went forth to
meet the bridegroom.
And five of them were wise, and five were foolish.

25:1–2

Well done, thou good and faithful servant . . . enter
thou into the joy of thy lord. 25:21

Unto every one that hath shall be given, and he shall
have abundance: but from him that hath not shall be
taken away even that which he hath. 25:29

Cast ye the unprofitable servant into outer darkness.

25:30

And before him shall be gathered all nations: and he
shall separate them one from another, as a shepherd
divideth his sheep from the goats. 25:32

For I was an hungred, and ye gave me meat: I was
thirsty, and ye gave me drink: I was a stranger, and ye
took me in:
Naked, and ye clothed me: I was sick, and ye visited
me: I was in prison, and ye came unto me. 25:35–36

Inasmuch as ye have done it unto one of the least of
these my brethren, ye have done it unto me. 25:40

There came unto him [Jesus] a woman having an
alabaster box of very precious ointment, and poured it
on his head, as he sat at meat. 26:7

To what purpose is this waste? 26:8

For ye have the poor always with you; but me ye have
not always. 26:11

What will ye give me, and I will deliver him unto you?
And they covenanted with him for thirty pieces of
silver. 26:15

My time is at hand. 26:18

Verily I say unto you, that one of you shall betray me.
26:21

And they were exceeding sorrowful, and began every
one of them to say unto him, Lord, is it I? 26:22

It had been good for that man [Judas] if he had not
been born. 26:24

Jesus took bread, and blessed it, and brake it, and gave
it to the disciples, and said, Take, eat; this is my body.
And he took the cup, and gave thanks, and gave it to
them, saying, Drink ye all of it;
For this is my blood of the new testament, which is
shed for many for the remission of sins.
But I say unto you, I will not drink henceforth of this
fruit of the vine, until that day when I drink it new
with you in my Father's kingdom. 26:26–29

My soul is exceeding sorrowful, even unto death. 26:38

O my Father, if it be possible, let this cup pass from
me: nevertheless, not as I will, but as thou wilt. 26:39

Could ye not watch with me one hour?
Watch and pray, that ye enter not into temptation: the
spirit indeed is willing, but the flesh is weak. 26:40–41

Behold, the hour is at hand, and the Son of man is
betrayed into the hands of sinners. 26:45

He came to Jesus, and said, Hail, Master; and kissed
him. 26:49

All they that take the sword shall perish with the
sword. 26:52

Thy speech bewrayeth thee. 26:73

Then began he to curse and to swear, saying, I know
not the man. And immediately the cock crew.
And Peter remembered the word of Jesus . . . Before
the cock crow, thou shalt deny me thrice. And he
went out, and wept bitterly. 26:74–75

The potter's field, to bury strangers in. 27:7

Have thou nothing to do with that just man. 27:19

Let him be crucified. 27:22

[Pilate] took water, and washed his hands before the multitude, saying, I am innocent of the blood of this just person: see ye to it. 27:24

His blood be on us, and on our children. 27:25

A place called Golgotha, that is to say, a place of a skull. 27:33

This is Jesus the King of the Jews. 27:37

He saved others; himself he cannot save. 27:42

Eli, Eli, lama sabachthani? that is to say, My God, my God, why hast thou forsaken me? 27:46

And, behold, the veil of the temple was rent in twain from the top to the bottom; and the earth did quake, and the rocks rent. 27:51

His countenance was like lightning, and his raiment white as snow. 28:3

Go ye therefore, and teach all nations, baptizing them in the name of the Father, and of the Son, and of the Holy Ghost. 28:19

Lo, I am with you alway, even unto the end of the world. 28:20

THE GOSPEL ACCORDING TO SAINT MARK

There cometh one mightier than I after me, the latchet of whose shoes I am not worthy to stoop down and unloose. 1:7

Arise, and take up thy bed, and walk. 2:9

The sabbath was made for man, and not man for the sabbath. 2:27

If a house be divided against itself, that house cannot stand. 3:25

The earth bringeth forth fruit of herself; first the blade, then the ear, after that the full corn in the ear.
4:28

What manner of man is this? 4:41

They came . . . into the country of the Gadarenes. 5:1

My name is Legion: for we are many. 5:9

And the unclean spirits went out, and entered the swine: and the herd ran violently down a steep place into the sea . . . and were choked in the sea. 5:13

Clothed, and in his right mind. 5:15

My little daughter lieth at the point of death. 5:23

Knowing in himself that virtue had gone out of him.
5:30

I see men as trees, walking. 8:24

Lord, I believe; help thou mine unbelief. 9:24

Suffer the little children to come unto me, and forbid them not; for of such is the kingdom of God. 10:14

Which devour widows' houses, and for a pretense
make long prayers. *12:40*

And there came a certain poor widow, and she threw
in two mites. *12:42*

Watch ye therefore: for ye know not when the master
of the house cometh, at even, or at midnight, or at the
cockcrowing, or in the morning:
Lest coming suddenly he find you sleeping. *13:35–36*

He is risen. *16:6*

Go ye into all the world, and preach the gospel to
every creature. *16:15*

THE GOSPEL ACCORDING TO SAINT LUKE

Hail, thou that art highly favored, the Lord is with
thee: blessed art thou among women. *1:28*

For with God nothing shall be impossible. *1:37*

Blessed is the fruit of thy womb. *1:42*

My soul doth magnify the Lord. *1:46*

For he hath regarded the low estate of his
handmaiden: for, behold, from henceforth all
generations shall call me blessed. *1:48*

He hath scattered the proud in the imagination of
their hearts.
He hath put down the mighty from their seats, and
exalted them of low degree. *1:51–52*

He hath filled the hungry with good things; and the
rich he hath sent empty away. *1:53*

Blessed be the Lord God of Israel; for he hath visited
and redeemed his people. *1:68*

As he spake by the mouth of his holy prophets, which
have been since the world began:
That we should be saved from our enemies, and from
the hand of all that hate us. *1:70–71*

Through the tender mercy of our God; whereby the
dayspring from on high hath visited us,
To give light to them that sit in darkness and in the
shadow of death. *1:78–79*

And she brought forth her firstborn son, and wrapped
him in swaddling clothes, and laid him in a manger;
because there was no room for them in the inn. 2:7

There were in the same country shepherds abiding in
the field, keeping watch over their flock by night.
And, lo, the angel of the Lord came upon them, and
the glory of the Lord shone round about them: and
they were sore afraid.
And the angel said unto them, Fear not: for, behold, I
bring you good tidings of great joy, which shall be to
all people.
For unto you is born this day in the city of David a
Savior, which is Christ the Lord. 2:8–11

Glory to God in the highest, and on earth peace,
good will toward men. 2:14

Lord, now lettest thou thy servant depart in peace.
2:29

A light to lighten the Gentiles, and the glory of thy
people Israel. 2:32

Wist ye not that I must be about my Father's business?
2:49

Jesus increased in wisdom and stature, and in favor
with God and man. 2:52

[The devil] showed unto him all the kingdoms of the
world in a moment of time. 4:5

For it is written, He shall give his angels charge over
thee, to keep thee:
And in their hands they shall bear thee up, lest at any
time thou dash thy foot against a stone. 4:10–11

Physician, heal thyself. 4:23

Woe unto you, when all men shall speak well of you!
6:26

Her sins, which are many, are forgiven; for she loved
much. 7:47

And he said to the woman, Thy faith hath saved thee;
go in peace. 7:50

Nothing is secret, that shall not be made manifest.
8:17

No man, having put his hand to the plow, and looking
back, is fit for the kingdom of God. 9:62

Nor scrip, nor shoes. 10:4

Peace be to this house. 10:5

The laborer is worthy of his hire. 10:7

I beheld Satan as lightning fall from heaven. 10:18

Many prophets and kings have desired to see those
things which ye see, and have not seen them; and to
hear those things which ye hear, and have not heard
them. 10:24

A certain man went down from Jerusalem to Jericho,
and fell among thieves. 10:30

A certain Samaritan . . . had compassion on him. 10:33

Go, and do thou likewise. 10:37

But Martha was cumhered about much serving. 10:40

But one thing is needful: and Mary hath chosen that good part, which shall not be taken away from her.

10:42

This is an evil generation: they seek a sign. 11:29

Soul, thou hast much goods laid up for many years; take thine ease, eat, drink, and be merry. 12:19

Thou fool, this night thy soul shall be required of thee. 12:20

Let your loins be girded about, and your lights burning. 12:35

For unto whomsoever much is given, of him shall be much required: and to whom men have committed much, of him they will ask the more. 12:48

The poor, and the maimed, and the halt, and the blind. 14:21

Which of you, intending to build a tower, sitteth not down first, and counteth the cost, whether he have sufficient to finish it? 14:28

Rejoice with me; for I have found my sheep which
was lost. *15:6*

[The prodigal son] wasted his substance with riotous
living. *15:13*

Bring hither the fatted calf, and kill it. *15:23*

For this my son was dead, and is alive again; he was
lost, and is found. *15:24*

Son, thou art ever with me, and all that I have is thine.
15:31

What shall I do? . . . I cannot dig; to beg I am
ashamed. *16:3*

The children of this world are in their generation
wiser than the children of light. *16:8*

He that is faithful in that which is least is faithful also
in much: and he that is unjust in the least is unjust also
in much. *16:10*

The beggar died, and was carried by the angels into Abraham's bosom. *16:22*

Between us and you there is a great gulf fixed. *16:26*

It were better for him that a millstone were hanged about his neck, and he cast into the sea. *17:2*

The kingdom of God is within you. *17:21*

Remember Lot's wife. *17:32*

Two men went up into the temple to pray; the one a Pharisee, and the other a publican. *18:10*

God, I thank thee, that I am not as other men are. *18:11*

God be merciful to me a sinner. *18:13*

Out of thine own mouth will I judge thee. *19:22*

If these should hold their peace, the stones would immediately cry out. *19:40*

He is not a God of the dead, but of the living. 20:38

In your patience possess ye your souls. 21:19

The Son of man coming in a cloud with power and
great glory. 21:27

This do in remembrance of me. 22:19

Not my will, but thine, be done. 22:42

For if they do these things in a green tree, what shall
be done in the dry? 23:31

The place, which is called Calvary. 23:33

Father, forgive them; for they know not what they do.
23:34

Lord, remember me when thou comest into thy
kingdom. 23:42

To day shalt thou be with me in paradise. 23:43

Father, into thy hands I commend my spirit. 23:46

He gave up the ghost. 23:46

He was a good man, and a just. 23:50

Why seek ye the living among the dead? 24:5

Their words seemed to them as idle tales. 24:11

Did not our heart burn within us, while he talked with
us? 24:32

The Lord is risen indeed. 24:34

THE GOSPEL ACCORDING TO SAINT JOHN

In the beginning was the Word, and the Word was
with God, and the Word was God. 1:1

And the light shineth in darkness; and the darkness
comprehended it not. 1:5

There was a man sent from God, whose name was
John. *1:6*

The true Light, which lighteth every man that cometh
into the world. *1:9*

The Word was made flesh, and dwelt among
us . . . full of grace and truth. *1:14*

No man hath seen God at any time. *1:18*

Behold the Lamb of God, which taketh away the sin
of the world. *1:29*

Can there any good thing come out of Nazareth? *1:46*

Hereafter ye shall see heaven open, and the angels of
God ascending and descending upon the Son of man.

1:51

Woman, what have I to do with thee? mine hour is
not yet come. *2:4*

The water that was made wine. *2:9*

This beginning of miracles did Jesus in Cana of Galilee, and manifested forth his glory; and his disciples believed on him. 2:11

When he had made a scourge of small cords, he drove them all out of the temple. 2:15

Make not my Father's house an house of merchandise. 2:16

Except a man be born again, he cannot see the kingdom of God. 3:3

The wind bloweth where it listeth, and thou hearest the sound thereof, but canst not tell whence it cometh, and whither it goeth: so is every one that is born of the Spirit. 3:8

How can these things be? 3:9

God so loved the world, that he gave his only begotten Son, that whosoever believeth in him should not perish, but have everlasting life. 3:16

There cometh a woman of Samaria to draw water:
Jesus saith unto her, Give me to drink. *4:7*

The hour cometh, and now is, when the true
worshippers shall worship the Father in spirit and in
truth. *4:23*

He was a burning and a shining light. *5:35*

Search the scriptures. *5:39*

What are they among so many? *6:9*

Gather up the fragments that remain, that nothing be
lost. *6:12*

I am the bread of life: he that cometh to me shall
never hunger; and he that believeth on me shall never
thirst. *6:35*

It is the spirit that quickeneth; the flesh profiteth
nothing. *6:63*

Judge not according to the appearance. *7:24*

Never man spake like this man. 7:46

He that is without sin among you, let him first cast a stone at her. 8.7

Neither do I condemn thee: go, and sin no more. 8:11

I am the light of the world: he that followeth me shall not walk in darkness, but shall have the light of life.

8:12

The truth shall make you free. 8:32

Ye are of your father the devil . . . there is no truth in him. . . . he is a liar, and the father of it. 8:44

I must work the works of him that sent me, while it is day: the night cometh, when no man can work 9.4

Whether he be a sinner or no, I know not: one thing I know, that, whereas I was blind, now I see. 9:25

I am the door. 10:9

I am come that they might have life, and that they
might have it more abundantly. 10:10

I am the good shepherd: the good shepherd giveth his
life for the sheep. 10:11

Other sheep I have, which are not of this fold. 10:16

I am the resurrection, and the life: he that believeth in
me, though he were dead, yet shall he live:
And whosoever liveth and believeth in me shall never
die. 11:25–26

Jesus wept. 11:35

It is expedient for us, that one man should die for the
people. 11:50

Then saith one of his disciples, Judas Iscariot, Simon's
son, which should betray him,
Why was not this ointment sold for three hundred
pence, and given to the poor? 12:4–5

Yet a little while is the light with you. Walk while ye
have the light, lest darkness come upon you. 12:35

That thou doest, do quickly. 13:27

A new commandment I give unto you, That ye love one another. 13:34

Let not your heart be troubled: ye believe in God, believe also in me.
In my Father's house are many mansions: if it were not so, I would have told you. I go to prepare a place for you. 14:1 2

I will come again, and receive you unto myself; that where I am, there ye may be also. 14:3

I am the way, the truth, and the life. 14:6

I will not leave you comfortless. 14:18

Peace I leave with you, my peace I give unto you: not as the world giveth, give I unto you. Let not your heart be troubled, neither let it be afraid. 14:27

Greater love hath no man than this, that a man lay down his life for his friends. 15:13

Ye have not chosen me, but I have chosen you. *15:16*

Whither goest thou? *16:5*

Ask, and ye shall receive, that your joy may be full.
16:24

Be of good cheer; I have overcome the world. *16:33*

Pilate saith unto him, What is truth? *18:38*

Now Barabbas was a robber. *18:40*

Behold the man! *19:5*

Woman, behold thy son! *19:26*

It is finished. *19:30*

Touch me not. *20:17*

Then saith he to Thomas . . . be not faithless, but
believing. *20:27*

Blessed are they that have not seen, and yet have
believed. 20:29

THE ACTS OF THE APOSTLES

Suddenly there came a sound from heaven as of a
rushing mighty wind. 2:2

There appeared unto them cloven tongues like as of
fire, and it sat upon each of them.
And they were all filled with the Holy Ghost, and
began to speak with other tongues. 2:3–4

Silver and gold have I none; but such as I have give I
thee. 3:6

And distribution was made unto every man according
as he had need. 4:35

If this counsel or this work be of men, it will come to
nought:
But if it be of God, ye cannot overthrow it. 5:38–39

Thy money perish with thee. 8:20

In the gall of bitterness, and in the bond of iniquity.

8:23

Saul, yet breathing out threatenings and slaughter against the disciples of the Lord. 9:1

Saul, Saul, why persecutest thou me? 9:4

It is hard for thee to kick against the pricks. 9:5

He is a chosen vessel unto me. 9:15

Immediately there fell from his eyes as it had been scales. 9:18

What God hath cleansed, that call not thou common.

10:15

God is no respecter of persons. 10:34

The gods are come down to us in the likeness of men.

14:11

We also are men of like passions with you. 14:15

Come over into Macedonia, and help us. *16:9*

Certain lewd fellows of the baser sort. *17:5*

Ye men of Athens, I perceive that in all things ye are
too superstitious.
For as I passed by, and beheld your devotions, I found
an altar with this inscription, TO THE UNKNOWN
GOD. *17:22–23*

God that made the world, and all things therein,
seeing that he is Lord of heaven and earth, dwelleth
not in temples made with hands;
Neither is worshipped with men's hands, as though he
needed any thing, seeing he giveth to all life, and
breath, and all things;
And hath made of one blood all nations of men for to
dwell on all the face of the earth. *17:24–26*

For in him we live, and move, and have our being; as
certain also of your own poets have said, For we are
also his offspring. *17:28*

Your blood be upon your own heads. *18:6*

And Gallio, cared for none of those things. *18:17*

Mighty in the Scriptures. *18:24*

We have not so much as heard whether there be any
Holy Ghost. *19:2*

All with one voice about the space of two hours cried
out, Great is Diana of the Ephesians. *19:34*

It is more blessed to give than to receive. *20:35*

I [Paul] am . . . a Jew of Tarsus, a city in Cilicia, a
citizen of no mean city. *21:39*

Brought up in this city at the feet of Gamaliel. *22:3*

And the chief captain answered, With a great sum
obtained I this freedom. And Paul said, But I was free
born. *22:28*

God shall smite thee, thou whited wall. *23:3*

Revilest thou God's high priest? *23:4*

I [Paul] am a Pharisee, the son of a Pharisee. *23:6*

A conscience void of offense toward God, and toward men. 24:16

When I have a convenient season, I will call for thee. 24:25

I appeal unto Caesar. 25:11

Paul, thou art beside thyself; much learning doth make thee mad. 26:24

I am not mad . . . but speak forth the words of truth and soberness. 26:25

For this thing was not done in a corner. 26:26

Almost thou persuadest me to be a Christian. 26:28

THE EPISTLE OF PAUL THE APOSTLE TO THE ROMANS

Wherein thou judgest another, thou condemnest thyself. 2:1

These, having not the law, are a law unto themselves.

2:14

The things that are more excellent. 2:18

Where no law is, there is no transgression. 4:15

Who against hope believed in hope. 4:18

Where sin abounded, grace did much more abound.

5:20

Death hath no more dominion over him. 6:9

I speak after the manner of men. 6:19

The wages of sin is death; but the gift of God is
eternal life. 6:23

The good that I would I do not: but the evil which I
would not, that I do. 7:19

Who shall deliver me from the body of this death?

7:24

Heirs of God, and joint-heirs with Christ. 8:17

For we know that the whole creation groaneth and
travaileth in pain together until now. 8:22

All things work together for good to them that love
God. 8:28

For whom he did foreknow, he also did predestinate
to be conformed to the image of his Son, that he
might be the firstborn among many brethren.
Moreover whom he did predestinate, them he also
called: and whom he called, them he also justified·
and whom he justified, them he also glorified. 8:29–30

If God be for us, who can be against us? 8:31

Who shall lay any thing to the charge of God's elect?
It is God that justifieth. 8:33

Who shall separate us from the love of Christ? 8:35

Neither death, nor life, nor angels, nor principalities,
nor powers, nor things present, nor things to come,
Nor height, nor depth, nor any other creature, shall
be able to separate us from the love of God, which is
in Christ Jesus our Lord. *8:38–39*

Hath not the potter power over the clay, of the same
lump to make one vessel unto honor, and another
unto dishonor? *9:21*

For who hath known the mind of the Lord? *11:34*

I beseech you therefore, brethren . . . that ye present
your bodies a living sacrifice, holy, acceptable unto
God, which is your reasonable service. *12:1*

Let love be without dissimulation. *12:9*

Be kindly affectioned one to another with brotherly
love. *12:10*

Given to hospitality. *12:13*

Be not wise in your own conceits.
Recompense to no man evil for evil. *12:16–17*

If it be possible, as much as lieth in you, live
peaceably with all men. *12:18*

Vengeance is mine; I will repay, saith the Lord. *12:19*

Be not overcome of evil, but overcome evil with good.
12:21

The powers that be are ordained of God. *13:1*

Render therefore to all their dues: tribute to whom
tribute is due; custom to whom custom; fear to whom
fear; honor to whom honor.
Owe no man anything, but to love one another. *13:7–8*

Love is the fulfilling of the law. *13:10*

The night is far spent, the day is at hand: let us
therefore cast off the works of darkness, and let us put
on the armor of light.
Let us walk honestly, as in the day; not in rioting and
drunkenness, not in chambering and wantonness, not
in strife and envying.
But put ye on the Lord Jesus Christ, and make
not provision for the flesh, to fulfil the
lusts thereof. *13:12–14*

Doubtful disputations. *14:1*

Let every man be fully persuaded in his own mind.
14:5

For none of us liveth to himself, and no man dieth to
himself.
For whether we live, we live unto the Lord; and
whether we die, we die unto the Lord: whether we
live therefore, or die, we are the Lord's. *14:7–8*

Let us therefore follow after the things which make
for peace. *14:19*

We then that are strong ought to bear the infirmities
of the weak, and not to please ourselves. *15:1*

*THE FIRST EPISTLE OF PAUL THE APOSTLE TO THE
CORINTHIANS*

God hath chosen the foolish things of the world to
confound the wise; and God hath chosen the weak
things of the world to confound the things which are
mighty. *1:27*

As it is written, Eye hath not seen, nor ear heard. 2:9

I have planted, Apollos watered; but God gave the increase. 3:6

We are laborers together with God: ye are God's husbandry. 3:9

Every man's work shall be made manifest: for the day shall declare it, because it shall be revealed by fire; and the fire shall try every man's work of what sort it is. 3:13

For the temple of God is holy, which temple ye are. 3:17

We are made a spectacle unto the world, and to angels, and to men. 4:9

Absent in body, but present in spirit. 5:3

A little leaven leaveneth the whole lump. 5:6

For even Christ our Passover is sacrificed for us. 5:7

It is better to marry than to burn. *7:9*

The fashion of this world passeth away. *7:31*

Knowledge puffeth up, but charity edifieth. *8:1*

I am made all things to all men. *9:22*

Know ye not that they which run in a race run all, but one receiveth the prize? *9:24*

Let him that thinketh he standeth take heed lest he fall. *10:12*

All things are lawful for me, but all things are not expedient. *10:23*

The earth is the Lord's, and the fullness thereof. *10:26*

If a woman have long hair, it is a glory to her. *11:15*

Take, eat: this is my body, which is broken for you: this do in remembrance of me. *11:24*

This cup is the new testament in my blood: this do ye,
as oft as ye drink it, in remembrance of me. *11:25*

Though I speak with the tongues of men and of
angels, and have not charity, I am become as sounding
brass, or a tinkling cymbal. *13:1*

Though I have all faith, so that I could remove
mountains, and have not charity, I am nothing.
And though I bestow all my goods to feed the poor,
and though I give my body to be burned, and have
not charity, it profiteth me nothing.
Charity suffereth long, and is kind; charity envieth
not, charity vaunteth not itself, is not puffed up. *13:2–4*

Beareth all things, believeth all things, hopeth all
things, endureth all things.
Charity never faileth. *13:7–8*

We know in part, and we prophesy in part.
But when that which is perfect is come, then that
which is in part shall be done away.
When I was a child, I spake as a child, I understood as
a child, I thought as a child: but when I became a
man, I put away childish things.

For now we see through a glass, darkly; but then face
to face: now I know in part; but then shall I know
even as also I am known.
And now abideth faith, hope, charity, these three; but
the greatest of these is charity. *13:9–13*

If the trumpet give an uncertain sound, who shall
prepare himself to the battle? *14:8*

Let all things be done decently and in order. *14:40*

And last of all he was seen of me also, as of one born
out of due time.
For I am the least of the apostles, that am not meet to
be called an apostle, because I persecuted the church
of God.
But by the grace of God I am what I am. *15:8–10*

But now is Christ risen from the dead, and become the
firstfruits of them that slept.
For since by man came death, by man came also the
resurrection of the dead.
For as in Adam all die, even so in Christ shall all be
made alive. *15:20–22*

The last enemy that shall be destroyed is death. *15:26*

Evil communications corrupt good manners. *15:33*

Thou fool, that which thou sowest is not quickened,
except it die. *15:36*

One star differeth from another star in glory. *15:41*

It is sown in corruption; it is raised in incorruption.
15:42

The first man is of the earth, earthy. *15:47*

Behold, I show you a mystery; We shall not all sleep,
but we shall all be changed,
In a moment, in the twinkling of an eye, at the last
trump: for the trumpet shall sound, and the dead shall
be raised incorruptible, and we shall be changed.
For this corruptible must put on incorruption, and this
mortal must put on immortality. *15:51–53*

Death is swallowed up in victory.
O death, where is thy sting? O grave, where is thy
victory? *15:54–55*

Watch ye, stand fast in the faith, quit you like men, be
strong. *16:13*

If any man love not the Lord Jesus Christ, let him be
Anathema Maranatha. *16:22*

THE SECOND EPISTLE OF PAUL THE APOSTLE TO THE CORINTHIANS

Not of the letter, but of the spirit: for the letter
killeth, but the spirit giveth life. *3:6*

Seeing then that we have such hope, we use great
plainness of speech. *3:12*

The things which are seen are temporal; but the
things which are not seen are eternal. *4:18*

We walk by faith, not by sight. *5:7*

Now is the accepted time. *6:2*

By honor and dishonor, by evil report and good
report. *6:8*

As having nothing, and yet possessing all things. 6:10

God loveth a cheerful giver. 9:7

Though I be rude in speech. 11:6

For ye suffer fools gladly, seeing ye yourselves are wise. 11:19

Forty stripes save one. 11:24

A thorn in the flesh. 12:7

My strength is made perfect in weakness. 12:9

The grace of the Lord Jesus Christ, and the love of God, and the communion of the Holy Ghost, be with you all. 13:14

THE EPISTLE OF PAUL THE APOSTLE TO THE GALATIANS

The right hands of fellowship. 2:9

Weak and beggarly elements. *4:9*

It is good to be zealously affected always in a good thing. *4:18*

Ye are fallen from grace. *5:4*

For the flesh lusteth against the Spirit, and the Spirit against the flesh: and these are contrary the one to the other: so that ye cannot do the things that ye would.

5:17

The fruit of the Spirit is love, joy, peace, long-suffering, gentleness, goodness, faith, Meekness, temperance. *5:22–23*

Every man shall bear his own burden. *6:5*

Be not deceived; God is not mocked: for whatsoever a man soweth, that shall he also reap. *6:7*

Let us not be weary in well doing. *6:9*

THE EPISTLE OF PAUL THE APOSTLE TO THE EPHESIANS

To be strengthened with might by his Spirit in the
inner man. *3:16*

Carried about with every wind of doctrine. *4:14*

We are members one of another.
Be ye angry, and sin not: let not the sun go down
upon your wrath. *4:25–26*

Speaking to yourselves in psalms and hymns and
spiritual songs, singing and making melody in your
heart to the Lord. *5:19*

Put on the whole armor of God. *6:11*

For we wrestle not against flesh and blood, but against
principalities, against powers, against the rulers of the
darkness of this world, against spiritual wickedness in
high places.
Wherefore take unto you the whole armor of God,
that ye may be able to withstand in the evil day, and
having done all, to stand. *6:12–13*

THE EPISTLE OF PAUL THE APOSTLE TO THE PHILIPPIANS

To live is Christ, and to die is gain. 1:21

Work out your own salvation with fear and trembling.
2:12

For it is God which worketh in you both to will and
to do of his good pleasure. 2:13

This one thing I do, forgetting those things which are
behind, and reaching forth unto those things which
are before,
I press toward the mark. 3:13–14

Whose end is destruction, whose God is their belly,
and whose glory is in their shame, who mind earthly
things. 3:19

The peace of God, which passeth all understanding,
shall keep your hearts and minds through
Christ Jesus. 4:7

Whatsoever things are true, whatsoever things are honest, whatsoever things are just, whatsoever things are pure, whatsoever things are lovely, whatsoever things are of good report; if there be any virtue, and if there be any praise, think on these things. 4:8

I have learned, in whatsoever state I am, therewith to be content. 4:11

THE EPISTLE OF PAUL THE APOSTLE TO THE COLOSSIANS

By him were all things created, that are in heaven, and that are in earth, visible and invisible . . . all things were created by him, and for him: And he is before all things, and by him all things consist. 1:16-17

Touch not; taste not; handle not. 2:21

Set your affection on things above, not on things on the earth. 3:2

Where there is neither Greek nor Jew, circumcision nor uncircumcision, Barbarian, Scythian, bond nor free: but Christ is all, and in all. 3:11

Fathers, provoke not your children to anger, lest they
be discouraged. *3:21*

Let your speech be alway with grace, seasoned with
salt. *4:6*

Luke, the beloved physician. *4:14*

THE FIRST EPISTLE OF PAUL THE APOSTLE TO THE THESSALONIANS

Labor of love. *1:3*

Study to be quiet, and to do your own business. *4:11*

The day of the Lord so cometh as a thief in the night.
5:2

Ye are all the children of light, and the children of the
day: we are not of the night, nor of darkness. *5:5*

Putting on the breastplate of faith and love; and for an
helmet, the hope of salvation. *5:8*

Pray without ceasing. 5:17

Prove all things; hold fast that which is good. 5:21

THE FIRST EPISTLE OF PAUL THE APOSTLE TO TIMOTHY

The law is good, if a man use it lawfully. 1:8

Christ Jesus came into the world to save sinners; of
whom I am chief. 1:15

For if a man know not how to rule his own house,
how shall he take care of the church of God? 3:5

Not greedy of filthy lucre. 3:8

Speaking lies in hypocrisy; having their conscience
seared with a hot iron. 4:2

Every creature of God is good, and nothing to be
refused, if it be received with thanksgiving. 4:4

Refuse profane and old wives' fables. 4:7

Let them learn first to show piety at home. 5:4

But if any provide not for his own, and specially for those of his own house, he hath denied the faith, and is worse than an infidel. 5:8

They learn to be idle, wandering about from house to house; and not only idle, but tattlers also and busybodies, speaking things which they ought not.
5:13

Drink no longer water, but use a little wine for thy stomach's sake. 5:23

We brought nothing into this world, and it is certain we can carry nothing out. 6:7

The love of money is the root of all evil. 6:10

Fight the good fight of faith, lay hold on eternal life.
6:12

Rich in good works. 6:18

O Timothy, keep that which is committed to thy trust, avoiding profane and vain babblings, and oppositions of science falsely so called. 6:20

THE SECOND EPISTLE OF PAUL THE APOSTLE TO TIMOTHY

For God hath not given us the spirit of fear; but of power, and of love, and of a sound mind. 1:7

A workman that needeth not to be ashamed. 2:15

Be instant in season, out of season. 4:2

I have fought a good fight, I have finished my course, I have kept the faith. 4:7

The Lord reward him according to his works. 4:14

THE EPISTLE OF PAUL TO TITUS

Unto the pure all things are pure. 1:15

THE EPISTLE OF PAUL TO PHILEMON

Making mention of thee always in my prayers. *1:4*

THE EPISTLE OF PAUL THE APOSTLE TO THE HEBREWS

Who maketh his angels spirits, and his ministers a
flame of fire. *1:7*

The word of God is quick, and powerful, and sharper
than any two-edged sword, piercing even to the
dividing asunder of soul and spirit, and of the joints
and marrow, and is a discerner of the thoughts and
intents of the heart. *4:12*

Strong meat belongeth to them that are of full age.

5:14

They crucify to themselves the Son of God afresh,
and put him to an open shame. *6:6*

Without shedding of blood is no remission. *9:22*

Faith is the substance of things hoped for, the
evidence of things not seen.   11:1

Wherefore seeing we also are compassed about with
so great a cloud of witnesses . . . let us run with
patience the race that is set before us,
Looking unto Jesus the author and finisher of our
faith.   12:1–2

Whom the Lord loveth he chasteneth.   12:6

The spirits of just men made perfect.   12:23

Let brotherly love continue
Be not forgetful to entertain strangers: for thereby
some have entertained angels unawares.   13:1–2

The Lord is my helper, and I will not fear what man
shall do unto me.   13:6

Jesus Christ the same yesterday, and to day, and for
ever.   13:8

For here have we no continuing city, but we seek on
to come.   13:14

To do good and to communicate forget not: for with
such sacrifices God is well pleased. *13:16*

THE GENERAL EPISTLE OF JAMES

Let patience have her perfect work, that ye may be
perfect and entire, wanting nothing.
If any of you lack wisdom, let him ask of God. *1:4–5*

Blessed is the man that endureth temptation: for when
he is tried, he shall receive the crown of life. *1:12*

Every good gift and every perfect gift is from above,
and cometh down from the Father of lights, with
whom is no variableness, neither shadow of turning.
1:17

Be swift to hear, slow to speak, slow to wrath:
For the wrath of man worketh not the righteousness
of God. *1:19–20*

Be ye doers of the word, and not hearers only. *1:22*

Unspotted from the world. *1:27*

As the body without the spirit is dead, so faith without works is dead also. 2:26

How great a matter a little fire kindleth! 3:5

The tongue can no man tame; it is an unruly evil. 3:8

This wisdom descendeth not from above, but is earthly, sensual, devilish. 3:15

Resist the devil, and he will flee from you. 4:7

What is your life? It is even a vapor, that appeareth for a little time, and then vanisheth away. 4:14

Be patient therefore, brethren, unto the coming of the Lord. Behold, the husbandman waiteth for the precious fruit of the earth, and hath long patience for it, until he receive the early and latter rain. 5:7

Ye have heard of the patience of Job. 5:11

The effectual fervent prayer of a right availeth much. 5:16

THE FIRST EPISTLE GENERAL OF PETER

Hope to the end. 1:13

The Father, who without respect of persons judgeth
according to every man's work. 1:17

All flesh is as grass, and all the glory of man as the
flower of grass. The grass withereth, and the flower
thereof falleth away:
But the word of the Lord endureth for ever. 1:24–25

Abstain from fleshly lusts, which war against the soul.
2:11

Honor all men. Love the brotherhood. Fear God.
Honor the king. 2:17

Ornament of a meek and quiet spirit. 3:4

honor unto the wife, as unto the weaker vessel.
3:7

Charity shall cover the multitude of sins. 4:8

A crown of glory that fadeth not away. 5:4

Be sober, be vigilant; because your adversary the devil,
as a roaring lion, walketh about, seeking whom he
may devour. 5:8

THE SECOND EPISTLE GENERAL OF PETER

And the day star arise in your hearts. 1:19

The dog is turned to his own vomit again. 2:22

THE FIRST EPISTLE GENERAL OF JOHN

God is light, and in him is no darkness at all. 1:5

If we say that we have no sin, we deceive ourselves,
and the truth is not in us. 1:8

If any man sin, we have an advocate with the Father,
Jesus Christ the righteous:
And he is the propitiation for our sins: and not
for ours only, but also for the sins of the
whole world. 2:1–2

He is antichrist, that denieth the Father and
the Son. 2:22

Whoso hath this world's good, and seeth his brother
have need, and shutteth up his bowels of compassion
from him, how dwelleth the love of God in him? 3:17

He that loveth not, knoweth not God; for God is
love. 4:8

There is no fear in love; but perfect love casteth out
fear. 4:18

THE GENERAL EPISTLE OF JUDE

Raging waves of the sea, foaming out their own
shame; wandering stars, to whom is reserved the
blackness of darkness for ever. 13

THE REVELATION OF SAINT JOHN THE DIVINE

I John, who also am your brother, and companion in tribulation, and in the kingdom and patience of Jesus Christ, was in the isle that is called Patmos, for the word of God, and for the testimony of Jesus Christ. *1:9*

What thou seest, write in a book, and send it unto the seven churches which are in Asia. *1:11*

And being turned, I saw seven golden candlesticks.
1:12

His feet like unto fine brass, as if they burned in a furnace; and his voice as the sound of many waters.
1:15

When I saw him, I fell at his feet as dead. *1:17*

I am he that liveth, and was dead; and, behold, I am alive for evermore, Amen; and have the keys of hell and of death. *1:18*

I have somewhat against thee, because thou hast left thy first love. *2:4*

To him that overcometh will I give to eat of the tree of life. 2:7

Be thou faithful unto death, and I will give thee a crown of life. 2:10

He shall rule them with a rod of iron. 2:27

I will give him the morning star. 2:28

I will not blot out his name out of the book of life. 3:5

I know thy works, that thou art neither cold nor hot: I would thou wert cold or hot.
So then because thou art lukewarm, and neither cold nor hot, I will spew thee out of my mouth. 3:15–16

Behold, I stand at the door, and knock. 3:20

The first beast was like a lion, and the second beast like a calf, and the third beast had a face as a man, and the fourth beast was like a flying eagle.
And the four beasts had each of them six wings about him; and they were full of eyes within: and they rest not day and night, saying, Holy, holy, holy, Lord God Almighty, which was, and is, and is to come. 4:7–8

Thou hast created all things, and for thy pleasure they
are and were created. 4:11

A book . . . sealed with seven seals. 5:1

He went forth conquering, and to conquer. 6:2

Behold a pale horse: and his name that sat on him was
Death, and Hell followed with him. 6:8

Four angels standing on the four corners of the earth,
holding the four winds of the earth. 7:1

Hurt not the earth, neither the sea, nor the trees. 7:3

All nations, and kindreds, and people, and tongues.
7:9

These are they which came out of great tribulation,
and have washed their robes, and made them white in
the blood of the lamb. 7:14

They shall hunger no more, neither thirst any more;
neither shall the sun light on them, nor any heat. 7:16

The name of the star is called Wormwood. 8:11

The kingdoms of this world are become the kingdoms
of our Lord and of his Christ. 11:15

There was war in heaven: Michael and his angels
fought against the dragon; and the dragon fought and
his angels,
And prevailed not. 12:7–8

The great dragon was cast out, that old serpent, called
the Devil, and Satan, which deceiveth the whole
world. 12:9

No man might buy or sell, save he that had the mark,
or the name of the beast. 13:17

The voice of many waters. 14:2

Babylon is fallen, is fallen, that great city. 14:8

Blessed are the dead which die in the Lord . . . that
they may rest from their labours. 14:13

And he gathered them together into a place called in
the Hebrew tongue Armageddon. *16:16*

He is Lord of lords, and King of kings. *17:14*

He treadeth the winepress of the fierceness and wrath
of Almighty God. *19:15*

Another book was opened, which is the book of life.
20:12

I saw a new heaven and a new earth: for the first
heaven and the first earth were passed away; and there
was no more sea.
And I John saw the holy city, new Jerusalem, coming
down from God out of heaven, prepared as a bride
adorned for her husband. *21:1--2*

God shall wipe away all tears from their eyes; and
there shall be no more death, neither sorrow, nor
crying, neither shall there be any more pain: for the
former things are passed away. *21:4*

There shall be no night there. *22:5*

He that is unjust, let him be unjust still: and he which
is filthy, let him be filthy still: and he that is righteous,
let him be righteous still: and he that is holy, let him
be holy still.
And, behold, I come quickly. 22:11–12

I am Alpha and Omega, the beginning and the end,
the first and the last. 22:13